Motive

Meet the Invisible Guest
in your wealth-biased relationships

Joe Strazzeri, Esq. CEPA

WRITTEN WITH JENNIFER SUMMER TOLMAN

Author: Joe Strazzeri, Strazzeri Mancini, LLP,
www.caretoknow.info

Written with: Jennifer Summer Tolman, Second Summer Inc.,
www.experiencesharedpurpose.net

Editor: Wendy Yorke, WRITE.EDIT.PUBLISH,
www.wendyyorke.com

Publisher: Serapis Bey Publishing, Arizona, USA,
www.serapisbeypublishing.com

Designer: Rebekka Mlinar, www.mlinar.nl

ISBN 979-8-9925723-9-1 (Hardcover)

Dedication

*This book is dedicated to Othership: the instinct
and drive to anticipate other people's needs, innovating to
serve and solve, often putting yourself second.*

Acknowledgements

None of the impactful work that we have achieved would have been possible without the amazing foundations that my parents gave me. My German, Iowa-farmgirl mother and my lovingly intense Sicilian immigrant father, both came from humble backgrounds to create the world where I grew up. My father taught me an unending work ethic combined with his forever quote, "Always ... take care of your family and put back a little of what you receive." Mom shared by example, an intuitive listening to find simple and clear underlying truths, along with her greatest strength of quietly being supportive without looking for credit.

Gratitude to my business partners, Steve Mancini, Shelley Lightfoot, Jeff Kates, Melisa Silverman, Dave Holaday, Carmen Bianchi, and Alex Matuk, for their continuous support. Steve, who is my best friend and mentor, helped me to find curiosity and a humble nature. Shelley, with her consistent reality check, helped me to push back and find clearer answers.

For my other mentors, whether they know they were mentoring me or not, (teachers, students, family, team members, and clients) who every week helped me see another perspective, question who I am and what I believe in, and celebrate the impact that we have on the lives we touch.

Annie and the kids, who taught me to accept people as they are and never be upset when people act like people. Cheerleaders and support no matter what life dealt me, but an honest mirror to my strengths and flaws with great vulnerability.

About the Author

Joe Strazzeri is an attorney and counselor to successful families and business owners. With a lifelong desire to become a lawyer, he leveraged his second career as a general contractor, hammering nails to pay for law school. He has been self-made since his 20s.

He is a founding partner in four companies that serve multi-generational affluent families and self-made business owners, and he teaches the trusted advisors to both. Their life's work centers on Three Systems of Family Thriving: family wealth, family relationships and family business relationships, and family advisory relationships. They focus on four key capabilities: tax masterminding, business succession, cleaning up messes in families' existing planning, and Family Synergy Work.

Over 25 years in business, he and his teams have counseled more than 750 eight- and nine-figure net worth families, and thousands of others. This experiential sample size renders the insights and perspectives shared in this book.

Joe credits his entrepreneurial tenacity to the dichotomy of his parents' origins. His mother a German, Iowa farmgirl, and his father, a crazy Sicilian entrepreneur, who began life as a teenage immigrant and drove the success of several real estate enterprises.

Joe cherishes time with his loving wife of 27 years, Annie, and their two adult children, Maddie and Sal. He enjoys life in the dual geographies of San Diego and Hawaii, and is often fly fishing with his business partner, Steve Mancini, his son Sal, and other members of their Strazzeri Mancini family.

About Jennifer Summer Tolman

I express my deep appreciation for the contributions Jennifer Summer Tolman and her firm have made to our practices and the creation of this book. In our current world, AI is used to 'create' communication that masquerades as original thought, where in reality it is the homogenization and regurgitation of other's thoughts. Jennifer, on the other hand, is a true thought partner who over this past decade has drawn out our best self and codified it into a better version of deeper and deeper thought. She has given us the ability to share what is important in a way that resonates with the families and their advisors that we are privileged to serve. Jennifer and I have also developed a deep mutual respect for each other and a lasting personal friendship.

Some people say that Steve, our teams, and I, have a knack for communicating and connecting. Converting those intimate moments to intellectual capital that I can share with countless families here from a printed page – that is an altogether different superpower. Families often call us in for counsel or counseling. Likewise, we call in professionals, all the time to partner in areas that are outside our wheelhouse and hence, our many years of partnering with Jennifer, her firm, and now through the book, Motive.

I also acknowledge our colleague and leader in the values-based planning space, Scott C. Fithian, for believing in Jennifer as a thinking partner early in her life's work, which enabled her to establish herself in this intellectual capital space, and to agree to make the journey with me these two decades later.

With gratitude,
Joe

Jennifer Summer Tolman has worked with Joe and his companies since 2016. Her creative services firm, Second Summer Inc., partners with upper echelon advisors and entrepreneurs who serve affluent self-made families. Jennifer's life's work is to identify intellectual capital her clients do not realize they have, articulate and package it, and intentionally attract Shared Purpose® relationships to their firms.

She is passionate about engaging brilliant advisors so their work together can help great families find their authentic advisory tribes. Her approach is equally applicable to capturing the intellectual capital of a family system.

Jennifer has focused on the white noise of this niche since 1996, and founded Second Summer Inc. in 2000. In 2006, she made the same journey with Scott C. Fithian for his book *The Right Side of the Table*. In 2009, she founded the Council for Shared Leadership, bringing together thought leaders and pioneers in the wealth coaching space, so that advisors and families could be students of the journey together.

Visit her at www.secondsummer.com

"Innovation comes from people realizing something that shoots holes in how they've been thinking about a problem."

Steve Jobs

Foreword

Before I met Joe the first time, I figured he was going to be another smart tax lawyer. Little did I realize how much I had to learn about him, yet more importantly, what I would learn from him as a business partner, mentor, and friend. I remember the first time he and I sat together with a family of significant wealth. What happened at that table was the foundation of a lifelong professional collaboration and a rare and precious friendship.

I watched him peel back the layers getting to the real reason we were all sitting there. Not the reason the meeting was allegedly called but the underlying drivers that mattered more. There were assets and complexities and plenty of choices for how to manage both. Joe unpacked all of that but he also looked behind the wealth, around it, and underneath it. He wanted to understand how the family first started thinking about things and how those drivers had morphed and evolved over time. He knew that if he could get to know the family, perhaps deeper than they even knew themselves, that's where the real planning would take shape.

Families long to have a team of trusted experts who like each other and who aren't trying to push against each other. Every advisor worth their salt talks the good talk of collaboration. The real test is how people behave when the family is not in the room. Joe talks about it all the time from the podium, but the difference is he actually lives it.

In my company and in my profession, I meet thousands of really smart investment and insurance advisors, tax and estate lawyers, CPAs, and other professionals. These folks are at the top of their game, exceedingly well-trained, brilliant, and incredibly caring. Their recommendations are sound, yet they often fail to communicate them in a way that resonates with matriarchs and patriarchs.

Joe is just as smart if not smarter than the next guy. What's vastly more important is that he cares about communicating in a way families are capable of processing. He believes they deserve to understand not just what they are doing but why they are doing it.

The families we are fortunate to work with know that if they pass along money without passing along wisdom, the two will soon part. Yet they don't always intuitively know how to unpack that part of planning. If you are reading this book, money's not the driver anymore. It's about being an effective steward of the assets and the relationships impacted by it. Joe's life's work gives families the keys to those undiscovered doors. The thresholds to deep understanding of who is in the room, why they are there, and what stands between their status quo and thriving.

This book gives families hope for a different way to be with family, wealth, and the advisors to both. Joe shows all of us how to take a deep and curious look at our own motives, and ultimately to discern what matters most.

Because of Joe, I have learned to be more collaborative with other professionals in our industry, even other professionals who do what I do. I have learned to play nicer in the sandbox. I have learned that details matter, and process matters just as much, if not more than the shiny object of a great strategy.

In my own companies, I have vastly exceeded what I thought was possible. And I give a lot of that credit to lessons I have learned from Joe.

Jeffrey Dunham, Founder

Dunham & Associates
Investments Counsel, Inc.
San Diego, CA

Dunham Trust Company
Reno, NV | Las Vegas, NV |
Cheyenne, WY

Praise for *Motive*
Reader Testimonials

"After reading *Motive*, I realized I needed to create some quiet time to contemplate and internalize what I just experienced. I found myself underlining and writing notes everywhere, realizing that I need to re-think a few things. *Motive* gave me the insights, encouragement, and tools to know that it's absolutely possible to create the positive family relationships and generational family legacy we all dream about."

Christopher Snider, CEPA®
CEO, Exit Planning Institute and Author of *Walking to Destiny – 11 Actions an Owner Must Take to Rapidly Grow Value & Unlock Wealth*

"I found myself reading *Motive* as the President of EPI yet simultaneously diving into it with my own life in my mind. In particular, the piece around The Four Phases of Family Thriving revealed a significant change in perspective for me. For the families and business our advisory community serves – and for me in my own family, business, and wealth – we all need advisors who understand and embrace the thinking in this book. *Motive* also offers keen insight into the deeper experience that next generation business owners are looking for – advisors who actually get to know their client families – or as Joe terms it, advisors who Care to Know™. It's about helping business owners know themselves more, their meaning, purpose, and their why. I especially recommend trying the Care to Know™ exercise in chapter five."

Scott Snider
President, Exit Planning Institute

"Joe helps us embrace the depth of impact that motive has on individual family members and family systems as a whole. He provides an entirely new way of looking at how people come to the table to solve problems and restore the deep connection that families crave. Joe helps us realize that in order to know another person the way we long to, we must set aside personal ego, and shift our perspective to curiosity. Motive gives us the path to navigate wealth-biased relationships and emerge thriving."

Carmen Bianchi
Past President of The Family Firm Institute
Past Faculty of the Fowler College of Business San Diego State University

---

"*Motive* invites you to slow down and recognize the unseen forces shaping every wealth-based relationship in your life. It's a guide to clarity, connection, and alignment, helping you shift from isolated roles to intentional partnerships. You won't just read this book. You'll think with it, wrestle with it, and return to it. It is a tool to reflect with, a companion to return to, and a resource that will help you lead with purpose for years to come."

Justin Goodbread
Keynote Speaker
Founder, Relentless Value Coaching
#1 Wall Street Journal Bestselling Author of *Your Baby's Ugly*
International Bestselling Author of *The Ultimate Sale*

"When offered the chance to be an early reader of *Motive*, I was immediately drawn to the content and subject matter. Throughout his life's work, and now in *Motive*, Joe takes complex business matters that originate in the heart and makes them approachable and understandable. He gets to the root cause of families' angst and pain, whereas many service providers are stuck on symptoms. *Motive* speaks to the core breakdowns in communication, and ultimately connection, that can impede legacy. More importantly, it teaches us what to do about it. Joe challenges his readers to truly get excited about who they work with, and if we are not – then he makes us think deeply about why we are engaged with an individual. This will become a new barometer for how I approach all relationships. It's a great reminder that we get to choose how we show up, who we partner and collaborate with, and what our end goals are. I am appreciative for the insights and impact this book is already making on my life."

Andrea Steinbrenner
Chief Executive Officer, Partner
Exit Consulting Group

"As advisors, we know in our hearts that there is so much more to our life's work than chasing the shiny object or financial return. *Motive* gave me pause to unpack what that really means, and to think deeply and intentionally about the power of authentic alignment in professional relationships. It made me realize how many conversations I've experienced where advisors – myself and others – already knew the answer. It gave me tools to rediscover curiosity as my own first reaction."

Gregory Banner
CFP®, CLU®, CRTP

"Reading *Motive* was a humbling and thought-provoking experience. Amid the noise and nonstop demands of the family office and investor space, I rarely find time for deep reflection.

The book shifted my perspective on family dynamics and governance. Instead of viewing these structures as rigid, Motive reframed them as living ecosystems where curiosity, compassion, and aligned purpose must drive the conversation. Joe's insights helped me rethink how I engage with families, not as a facilitator of answers but as a partner in progress who listens deeply and helps uncover the layers beneath long-standing patterns.

Motive is more than a book. It is a journal of behavioral insight and personal challenge that I know I will return to again and again."

Kathleen J. Tepley
Los Angeles Consulting Group

Contents

Introduction:
A Guide for Change and Progress

In the pages that follow, I have endeavored to create more of an experience than a traditional book. Some people will power through attempting a quick read, and others will find the popcorn of a new idea in the pauses we have carefully infused throughout.

One of my favorite mottos is, "Hope is a great conversation." Through a combination of compassionate sarcasm, tender truths, and dense prose, my hope is that families read for what they haven't heard and not what they already know. At times you'll find yourself rereading a sentence or a paragraph. When you do, please know that I have attempted to embed deeper nuance into those nuggets of compassion and contemplation.

Each chapter offers deep thinking exercises, audio overviews of our counseling concepts, and real client stories. In our decades of counseling and teaching families and advisors, we know that personal interaction with the material has a dramatic effect on the depth of influence, and the speed and durability of progress. Beyond reading or hearing a presentation, this deeper engagement helps families chip away at change. If you are holding an actual 3D book, versus an e-book, you'll find blank journal pages at the back on which to capture your thinking from the exercises. If you don't have a hard copy, you'll want to allocate a notebook or journal to do the work.

Across our multiple companies, my partners, teams, and I have a motto – Care to Know™. It reminds us to own curiosity as our first reaction, always seeking to learn more about what is right in front of us, and even more so, to bravely expose our own blind spots. That is my goal for the families and advisors reading this book. I say this from humility, not arrogance, as I do this work daily in my personal and professional relationships. Perfection is not my strong suit, but perseverance has a way of prevailing.

My mentor and colleague, Aaron Turner, founder of One Thought, has taught me that the way you relate to and process data and relationships has far greater impact on your experiences than the circumstances in front of you or facts on paper. State of mind is often invisible yet it's the domino to every (yes, every) relational and technical result. In my personal work with Aaron, I am consistently astonished at what I am capable of with a clearer mind. As he likes to say, "More lift, less drag. A clearer state of mind gives fuller access to the true power of the mind."

When the stakes are high in life and wealth, assumptions and foregone conclusions create the perception of a safe space to soldier on. In reality, the power of a clear, quiet mind allows radically better outcomes in families' technical wealth planning and their family, business, and advisory relationships. Your joy becomes more joyful. The friction you feel around material assets and cherished relationships dissipates, allowing ease to be your partner in progress. In my world, Care to Know™ is the state of mind that allows families and their trusted advisors to make this journey.

Henry Ford said, "If I had asked people what they wanted, they would have said faster horses." I believe that successful families and business owners tolerate far too much angst and pain in their material assets and cherished relationships. And that, if you are reading this, you deserve more than a faster horse. If you choose to meet motive, the Invisible Guest in your wealth-biased relationships, you will find a place of ease and celebration that may not currently seem possible.

Thank you for joining me here to begin the journey.

Best,
Joe

For digital access to all of Motive's audio overviews, please scan the QR codes next to their reference in this book.

Additionally, you can visit www.strazzerimancini.com/othership/#motive to access each of the audio overviews and exercises. You'll find a simple portal from which you can print the exercises and blank journal pages and listen to the audio files and complete the exercises.

Chapter 1

The Invisible Guest
in Wealth-biased Relationships

What if there was a fundamental misunderstanding in the relationships you cherish the most? The ones that are thriving because you have nourished, mentored, and loved them. And the ones you have damaged or regretfully failed to tend to, and perhaps those that have damaged you.

As humans, we think we know our people. We're certain of our tribe's behavioral drivers – their actions, reactions, missteps, and blind spots. Often, without bearing witness to an actual event, we know the truth about what they did and why they did it, including the foregone conclusion that they will do the same thing again. We tuck our carefully crafted perception of another's modus operandi into a black box labeled, Facts. We double lock the box and seal out the light of alternatives that don't match up with our framework.

Motives – yours, theirs, and the collective – are the chess pieces on the board of relationship. We like to think of motive as other peoples' stuff, often forgetting that every one of us is the other person in someone else's world.

Definition of Motive
- *Reason for doing something,*
  "She goes to the gym daily to stay fit."
- *Driver for behavior, decision, or action,*
  "He is always argumentative around Uncle Jim."
- *Object of a person's action,*
  "Her motive was unconditional love."

Wealth-Biased Relationships

Motive is alive and well in all relationships, yet affluence exaggerates individuals' behaviors and group dynamics. Whether it's the family's holiday table, the capital campaign gala, the C-Suite boardroom, or a meeting with trusted advisors, everyone has something to gain, lose, or protect.

Relationships impacted by wealth-bias

- *High-net-worth families (parents, kids, siblings, extended family).*
- *Family businesses (bloodline, non-bloodline).*
- *Professional advisors (financial, legal, tax, insurance, estate, governance).*
- *Philanthropic (donors, causes, planned giving officers).*

The Role of Misunderstanding

Relationships are made up of fact patterns, each a composite of factors outside of our control, and those that are highly controllable. The outcomes we experience are a collection of little choices, big choices, or not choosing at all. Fact patterns happen at the hands of humans, and inherently, the vast majority of patterns result in at least a tiny nuance of misunderstanding. To understand is to comprehend or interpret. A misunderstanding is the act of mistaken comprehension or wrong interpretation.

During more than two decades of teaching and counseling, Steve and I have observed that most conflict (yes, most) begins with a misunderstanding of previous facts and fact patterns. We're certain we know the nuance and details that preceded an action or outcome. Certainty is a dangerous frame around external circumstances, many of which we did not witness firsthand. Too often what we own as stone-cold truth is rooted in wrong interpretation.

Definition of Misunderstanding

Mis: incorrect, wrongly, mistaken. Converts a word to its opposite.
Understanding: comprehension, personal interpretation.
Misunderstanding: incorrect interpretation of action, intent, or fact pattern.

Motive's Workflow: You Are What You Think, and Others Are Too

Motive is a behavioral driver muddied in the past, stewing in the present, and projecting the future. It bears a predictable sequence, almost a workflow that goes something like this:

- **Event:** a thing happens, or a scenario presents itself.
- **Interpretation:** participants interpret the available facts firsthand, and those not present gather facts through third-hand, side-bar conversations.
- **Formation:** all parties leverage the power of hindsight to assimilate their conclusions.
- **Complication:** never one-dimensional, each conclusion is a composite of misunderstood prior facts – a solar system of assumptions with multiple orbits.
- **Misunderstanding:** wrongly interpreted facts and crucial missing data are converted to a back story of complete accuracy.
- **Assignment:** not only do we know what they did, we know why they did it.

HEAR FROM JOE: AUDIO OVERVIEW #1

7

Motive is what happens when you convert a hunch or belief system to an absolute truth. The collection of facts is molded into a concrete pillar of steadfast knowledge. You keep adding to the pillar over time, applying the paint and stucco of accumulated observations. More paint, more stucco. It is going so well, why not add a bejeweled crown? The pillar becomes a touchstone for feeling in control of your circumstances. It is a slippery slope from knowing what is true, to needing it to be true.

In reality, 99 per cent of the data that made its way into the workflow was a combination of misinterpreted data, or missing data invented to fill a void. We use too few facts and misunderstand the ones in front of us. Statisticians would have a field day with our inclination to predict and ascertain absolute truth without relevant probability.

And still, we are humans trying to be human. Our psyches are overloaded. We don't have the time or intellectual bandwidth to investigate every life event in search of complete transparency. Assigning motive gives us a fast track to conclusion, allowing our emotions the space to breathe. When perception and interpretation become calcified into the truth of the past, we have a safe way to make sense of present behavior and navigate a predictable future.

However, motive's prologue, misunderstanding, is nefarious, both righteous and sneaky. Not only do we know exactly what they did, we know why they did it. It is such a perfect package we don't want to pull the ribbon off. Unless of course, we prefer to become curious about the truth inside the black box of angst and pain.

HEAR FROM JOE: AUDIO OVERVIEW #2

When your message gets lost in your delivery

As usual, Sam is talking and thinking at the same time. He doesn't have the energy to use the neutral words and the careful delivery their counselor makes them practice out loud. He takes a clumsy stab at something he needs to communicate, using an edgy tone and a few loaded generalizations, such as 'always' and 'never'. Sally recoils. Without pausing to regroup, Sam tries again. Sally musters her own generalizations, yet hers are about Sam's tone and delivery, not the subject he was hoping to discuss.

Friction in relationships loves poor delivery, a sure fire path to explosion. Now, Sam and Sally are in a full-blown stand off and neither is sure what they are fighting about. The conflict is so muddied in Sam's poor delivery, they never got to the salient underlying subject. Even worse, the subject Sam hoped to address was buried deep in layer upon layer of prior misunderstanding.

Motive's Negativity Bias

Ironically, we assign motive to motive itself. We give it a bad rap, tangling it in negativity and grudge. Yet motives can be pure and passionate, such as love, empathy, or fear, and that someone will leave, get hurt, or hurt someone else.

Motive is simply a two-sided coin of data.

1. The passionate protection of a person, partnership, or precious asset.

2. The assessment of another's behavioral drivers, and assignment to a known cause.

So much of life and wealth is merely data – facts and fact patterns we use to interpret our experiences. In our teaching, counseling, and technical work we parse data into three distinct forms, No Data, Stated Data, and Verified Data. In the land of motive, No Data is the cycle of observe and assume, information assembled in a vacuum of dialogue or firsthand experience. Stated Data is taking what others say at face value, often backed up by history, and lacking deeper inquiry. It's often co-dependent, a feedback loop of seeking out opinions from those who are likely to agree with you. Validation lets you exhale, confirm, and move on. In the short term, it's faster and simpler than searching for opposing facts. In the long term, Stated Data is the raw material of misunderstanding. Verified Data is the fly fisherman's curiosity rod. When someone comes clean with an uncomfortable situation, we cast empathy long and far to learn their firsthand account of what transpired, and how they feel about their choices in hindsight. In all walks of life, quality of data correlates to quality of outcome. If we want to fully resolve a difficult scenario – a clean removal of hook from cheek – we need to slow down long enough to invite unknown truth into the present moment.

When someone you cherish is courageous enough to come clean with the muck of life, don't you owe it to them to meet courage with curiosity? If the roles were reversed, wouldn't you want your own truth to be met with a servant leader's heart and genuine interest? And if you were, might the safety of validation encourage you to come forward more often? Imagine if all members of a family wealth or family business system prioritized Verified Data. All that energy previously applied to the angst and pain of interpreting or assigning motive could be reallocated to cultivating a thriving future.

The Correlation Between Expertise and Reduced Outcomes

Families and their advisors are co-dependent in the use of expertise as a tool for power and efficiency. The expert is often beyond being questioned, achieving perceived efficiencies and tidy resolution. Meanwhile, the smarter, faster thinker suffers the most. You figure it all out at Mach speed. Clutching the obvious answers, you linger in the relational waiting room, enduring the excruciating pain of watching others' slow processing.

Expertise is the enemy of curiosity, giving some of us a hall pass to show up for important conversations unprepared. Practicing in the car on the way to the meeting, we muster our quest to convince and win, organizing facts into exactly the right pitch. Some people would argue that this is preparation, yet in reality it's the art of verifying a predetermined endgame. True preparation is the journey of getting your mind ready to receive, opening to unknown influences, and inviting others to poke holes in your hunches.

Hear this next part with a tender heart. The need to be seen as an expert shuts down your learning and limits the outcomes of the group. The more you know about a relational or technical topic, the more you forget to seek out what has changed, or what you have not yet learned. What if instead, you used all that time in the waiting room to muster your curiosity and question your conclusions? The most effective experts never believe what is in front of them. They are more inclined to inquire about their blind spots, variables, and nuance, rather than reaffirming the wisdom of their prior experience.

Hope is a Great Conversation

Understanding motive increases your awareness of your own behavior and opens you to exploring others'. Getting really clean in all of this is the key to unlocking the black box of angst and pain in cherished relationships, personally and professionally.

When you can authentically stand in the shoes of another's situation, you become partners in designing alternatives, both in understanding the past and navigating a mutual future. Entrepreneurs do this for customers and clients all the time. When the relationships are one step closer to home, it becomes harder to squeegee the fog from the glass.

You have been on the planet long enough to have muscle memory for what serves you well. Breaking apart the patterns triggers resistance that can be tough to soldier through. Next time you find yourself leaning into the art of knowing, pause and consider what game you are trying to win, and how the win will serve you long term. Are you seeking to convince yourself of what you already presume, or are you seeking to learn about, or understand someone or something? Remember that to see it - that little morsel in your blind spot - you have to want it. The search to convince gives you permission to close off possibilities which sadly walls you off from those people you most wish to be closer to.

If you can learn the sequence and nuance of action and reaction embedded in your cherished relationships, you become safe seeing into another's soul, allowing them to see a little more of yours. All those thought-nastics – the repeating routines of thinking gymnastics that you have spent a lifetime designing and perfecting – become the performances of the past.

The rewards for understanding motive are bountiful, transforming the righteous safety of self-convincing to an extremely stale donut. It is so clearly distasteful, you no longer have to resist temptation. True facts become easier to spot in yourself and others. Rehashing difficult scenarios is no longer necessary because there is no more joy in the proof-finding. Hope breeds resilience, letting us laugh at ourselves and love our tribes more than we ever thought possible.

Kathryn Dejong with Randy Newhard

"When we were first introduced to Joe more than 20 years ago, we had a few things on our plates. My stepdad, Randy, had founded the company and grown it to a certain point. I started working in the business as the receptionist when I was 18 years old, and I was working my way up the ladder. Randy was starting to think about how the business would continue after he wasn't working.

We didn't have college educations. We were a self-made, family-owned business growing the company through relationships. We cared about our employees because they had helped us make the business successful.

Joe had met with Randy and my mom initially. Randy wanted to identify who might be his successor. So, Joe came onsite and interviewed all the head managers. He wanted to get an idea of their personalities, their dedication, their loyalty, their humility, all of that.

I wasn't there that day, but Joe went into my office to leave me a note or something, and he saw all these pictures that I had of Randy's company when he first started. And I guess he was really taken by the fact that I had those photos. He could see that I had a real connection to the company and what Randy had built. So Joe asked Randy, "Did you ever think about your daughter?" And it turns out that Randy didn't feel I was in love with the company. In truth, there was no one there who loved that company more than I did, except for him.

Joe did all those interviews and saved me for the last. I thought maybe he didn't think my role was that important but it was actually the opposite. During that interview he asked me if I ever saw myself being the person to take over the business one day. I said, of course. That's what I've been building towards the whole time. But Randy and I had never talked about it. So that was when it all started coming together.

Joe began mentoring me for the things that I hadn't learned from my boots-on-the-ground experience. It was the bigger picture of understanding the financials and creating long term goals. All the stuff outside of day-to-day landscape and tree services. And on a parallel path he was advising Randy on how to protect his future financially.

When we met Joe, I had worked my way up to running the operations. The process unfolded with a lot of heavy questions that put me in my place. I felt like, I already know about this company. But a good mentor has a way of pulling things out of you. And so he set me on a path and helped me see, if I was serious about running the company someday, there was a lot I needed to learn. I reached out to our other advisors and dove into the depths of it as much as I could so that the succession would be a success.

That level of candor matters a lot. Being successful on your own is great, but when someone can recognize traits in you that you may not want to see, or maybe you're afraid to see them, or it's ego or whatever. There's a way of riding that line between honesty and empowerment to steer you on the right course. Throughout our relationship, I have always known Joe's intentions were meant for the company's success not his own gain. It was never just about business for me, and it wasn't for him either.

When Randy realized that I might be the successor, it was such a relief. There's nobody better to take it over than your family, your daughter. Like they say, blood's thicker than water. We've always had great people who cared about the company but nobody cares more than the family.

For us the most important thing to find in an advisory relationship is somebody that really wants to know your business, how it works, who's in there, what do you do, how do you do it. Someone that really understands, it's not just a business, it's our business.

I think a lot of business relationships, especially when they deal with wealth, tend to be transactional. But in self-made companies, there's nothing more personal than the company. When you're talking to an advisor and you're wanting them to understand how important it is to keep the legacy alive, you want someone who understands that.

Joe and his teams are rooted in that. They genuinely want to have deep conversations about what you're struggling with and what you want to see happen. Some people are fine making a little money. Some people want to make a lot. Some people want to give to their employees. Some people don't. Those seem like basic questions, but they're much deeper in self-made companies.

I sort of assume that anyone we're referred to as an advisor is smart, so then it becomes about the connection that you feel along with that. Having that sense of connection was a motivator for me because I felt accountable to the work we were doing together. If Joe hadn't taken a personal interest in me, I wouldn't have felt comfortable being candid about what I needed help with, or sharing what I wanted for my role and for the future of the company.

If we hadn't begun the journey with Joe and his companies 20 years ago, I don't know if we would have been as successful in our succession. I think we could have wound up with a successor who was more in it for their own financial gain. The employees that knew the company so well and were so loyal would have left over time. I don't think that we would have lasted forever, for 43 years so far."

BEFORE THE BRILLIANCE EXERCISE

Self-made matriarchs and patriarchs are really smart people. Their trusted advisors are best-in-class. All that IQ and instinct encourage and reward the bad behavior of assumption. Hunches about other peoples' actions have been proven right so often, jumping to conclusion is a coveted and treasured skill. It is enough to make you giddy until you stop and realize that the assumptions and assignments you make about others' motives are being made about you, by someone with your same superpower.

Think of a time when you felt wrongly accused, pigeon-holed, or blamed for something that mattered deeply. Use a journal or notebook to make notes about the scenario, the facts as you recall them, who was involved, and what assumptions were pinned to your behavior.

- What was assumed about you?
- What were the participants at risk of losing or in need of protecting?
- What did they stand to gain by being right?
- What was inaccurate or misunderstood?
- How did you feel in the moment?

The next step is to make notes about the drivers you brought to the situation. Be as self-honest as you can about both your healthy and unhealthy emotions at the time. Maybe there was a desire to protect someone from making a regretful choice or a need to prove someone else wrong as revenge for prior bad behavior.

- What were you vulnerable about?
- What did you need to protect?
- What did you need to defend?
- What outcome was non-negotiable?
- What was at stake if it didn't happen?

Take a few deep breaths and get ready for the good stuff. Review your notes from both sets of questions and look for parallels. Identify where, perhaps, you misunderstood their intentions. Motive's two-sided coin is often alive and well in a single situation.

MOTIVE'S HALL PASS EXERCISE

When we create a truism about someone else, we assign a motive. We dislike it when others typecast us, yet humans do it all the time to the people and events around them. Consider the hall pass you allow yourself when forming conclusions about other people's motives.

Think of a specific scenario in which something difficult transpired with a cherished relationship, and you know still, to this day, exactly what drove their behavior. It was painful for both of you but at least you knew where they were coming from. Or did you?

Select the bullets that feel true for you.

- It's not my first rodeo.
- I'm an exceptional judge of character.
- My gut instincts are usually spot on.
- They have been that way since I can remember.
- I don't have time to stop and over think it.

Now, let's play with the opposites. If someone whose respect and love mattered to you applied these justifications to their assumptions about your behavior, how might it feel?

Chapter 2

Choosing and Being Chosen

Explore with me a premise about which my business partner, Steve and I, are passionate. There is an uncanny correlation between the quality of your financial, legal, and tax advisory relationships, and the quality of the outcomes you derive from these relationships. The journey is not as simple as engaging the smartest advisor who is loved by your peers. It is surrounding yourself with a personal, right-fit wisdom tribe.

Technical and relational alignment have far greater impact on quantifiable planning outcomes than many families are aware of. Your advisors long to dig in deep with you. They want to meet you pound-for-pound with dynamic dialogue and debate. How you're doing and what you achieve matters to them. They care deeply about you, your family, and your business. When you give them more permission to come forth, their compassion and wisdom will radiate your way.

Pause for a moment and envision what it feels like to partner with an advisor who lights up from the work you do together. Someone with whom you have deep, professional chemistry, trust, and intimacy. Someone who is passionate about how you move the needle in other people's lives.

What if that person is already sitting across the table from you and you simply haven't allowed their full contribution into the room? It begs for one of our fondest mottos, "Hope is a great conversation."

What is Broken and Why Don't We Fix it?

When you wake up with the thrill of a wild hair idea, or sudden realization of a large undefined problem, who do you call? That familiar spark of your genius is alight with anticipation or concern – who is your must-share-it-with rock? Who is the one person on the planet who instantly understands you, loves your quirks, and feeds your ability to see the far side simultaneously?

Very few big thinkers I know have that rock. Their cups overflow with colleagues and partners, key people, and great friendships. Yet, when their intellectual capital is innovating at Mach speed, who can they rely on to share their bliss, seek clarity, and tire-kick for weak points? For many people, the question draws a blank.

What is it about our society that allows many of the hardest working minds in business and wealth to go it alone, either sometimes or all the time? Why don't we have a methodology to choreograph the dance of intellect between affluent families and professional advisors? And if we did, what specific characteristics define their ideal partners?

At one of our teaching forums, The Gathering, one of my intellectual rocks asked if she could pose questions to a self-made client who was speaking on a panel about business succession. She approached Jack and inquired, "It sounds like you found your true north of an advisory team later on in your business life. You lit up like a Christmas tree when you talked about them. Forgive me, but I couldn't help wondering, why didn't you refine and build your tribe decades ago?"

He seemed stuck: a deer in the headlights.

Finally, Jack replied, "Well, I had great internal advisors in my company all those years, and we did a lot of things ourselves, but I didn't know the possibility of having this kind of tribe even existed."

This is a true story, and although I am humbled and grateful to be among the advisors who light Jack up, I was saddened by his response. It told me that there are millions of self-made men and women – entrepreneurial families and professional advisors – who traverse their life's work surrounded by smart people, yet they lack that push-and-a-hug partnership that transforms rote planning into sheer possibility and better outcomes.

HEAR FROM JOE: AUDIO OVERVIEW #3

The Four Quadrants of Relational Dynamics
During more than two decades of teaching and client work together, Steve and I have noticed a troubling trend. People apply more intentionality to writing notes for their housekeeper than vetting and selecting their professional tribes. We specifically mean, the relationships between self-made entrepreneurs and high-net-worth families, and their professional advisors across all disciplines, including, financial, legal, and tax.

Let's explore the four quadrants of these relational dynamics.

Quadrant One: successful families and business owners choosing their advisors

My client, Jack, shared his insight. He lacked the ability to name the problem, and the process and path to solve it, the first domino toppling the next. If you can't frame the promise of a better way, how do you build criteria for seeking it?

Families often choose their advisors by trusting their gut. You meet a seemingly A+ player at a gala or on the golf course, or you are referred by a trusted ally. Working from this anecdotal endorsement, you hear the advisor's pitch and it resonates. Instinct has served you well in creating your wealth, and this landscape can't be all that different. Or is it?

Instinct feels like a methodology, yet it's only about 20 per cent of the success recipe for effective partnering. The other 80 per cent is comprised of the table stakes and the deal-breakers, the unexplored truths that lie in wait of their future reveal. All those aspects that no one asks about up front, offer row-on-row of dominoes, in wait for their topple at a future misunderstanding and misstep.

Importantly, it is no one's fault. The professional advisory industry doesn't offer up a defined methodology for selecting your right-fit partners, relationally and technically. There's no play book for designing your dream team criteria and vetting for transparent alignment. The crush of life puts enough competing demands on your bandwidth. You abdicate the mental gymnastics and do the best you can with what you have. You hire that A+ player and return to running your life and business.

Quadrant Two: successful families and business owners being chosen by advisors

Meanwhile, the selection process is well underway, hiding in plain sight. Even wealth that is bathed in humility has a public persona. People know you built a thriving enterprise or inherited a substantial nest egg. They notice the car you drive, places you travel, and clubs you frequent, and they join you in the first-class cabin. Money changes hands in the background, paying for golf, or compensating for an introduction, either literally, or quid pro quo. There is nothing inherently evil about networking. Advisors are building their client rosters exactly as families are building their businesses. The problem isn't ethics, it's awareness. Do you realize that your actions and habits are why you are chosen?

Quadrant Three: advisors choosing successful families and business owners

Great advisors, like my friend Susan, have a way of being out and about in the right circles to steadily grow their businesses. When she is engaged by a new family, she has a methodology for onboarding the client. However, there is a gap in discernment – after the courting – and prior to the hiring.

What are advisors like Susan's selection criteria for a right-fit client? Does she have them, and if the fit is wrong, does she back away, leaving financial and business rewards on the table? What is the demographic filter for those people who may derive the greatest value from her firm's expertise and service model? What relationship dynamics have the endurance to inspire them well into the twilight years of the long-term commitment they pushed across the planning table in search of a signature?

Fast-forward to her firm's third or fourth decade in business.

Do they still accept each and every family who willingly writes the proverbial check?

Like many seasoned, successful advisors, Susan's firm has achieved the enviable position of working exclusively by referral, from client families and advisory colleagues. We might ask firms like hers to look in the mirror and authentically answer the following two questions:

1. If a family to whom you are introduced doesn't light you up relationally, or they are not a fit demographically, how do you gracefully exit prior to engagement?
2. Or does the relationship proceed anyway?

How do all of the above factors influence the family's planning experiences, outcomes, and a firm's ability to thrive, to dig deep into its best work on the family's behalf?

Quadrant Four: advisors being chosen by successful families and business owners
Does the advisor ever wonder why they got the gig? Does the selection criteria that led to being hired align with the central aspects of joy and pride derived from their life's work? Does the family pursue the firm for its outsized market returns while, in truth, it's the planning and stewardship that actually created those outcomes? Were the families attracted by a big public win that's an outlier to the firm's preferred and primary business model?

Affluent families and high-end professional advisors are masters of their craft when it comes to vetting. Your eagle eyes of discernment are better than most. Yet, in the precious realm of choosing and being chosen, you check that bionic vision at the conference room door.

There is a direct correlation between how deeply advisors summon their best work, and how families partner in their relationships. Or how they don't. At times, advisors' biggest ideas remain dormant because their time and fees are too squeezed to develop the potentiality. Or they could place a toe in the waters of vulnerability to share an aha moment – yet, they pause shy of the risk – anticipating a soul-wounding shut down.

Across all four quadrants, and in both directions, these relationships have the power to transform lives and businesses. Yet, instead of digging into how, if, and whether you're fit to partner for the long-term, there's a premature lean into "Yes."

When families and advisors traverse the relational side of choosing and being chosen, their data falls into one of three buckets, as mentioned in Chapter 1, No Data, Stated Data, or Verified Data. No Data is the purview of golf and cocktails, perceptions and hunches. Stated Data is the love language of courting –what you say to each other, or what other people have told you. Verified Data comes from a place of deep contemplation. It relies on a tangible, selection criteria, and vetting process to reconcile the potential suitors against the filter. Verified Data has courage as its wingman, the guts to walk away, when saying Yes is so much easier.

The Fear of the Loss, the Joy of the Gain
Fear of loss of connection is a basic human trait. It's present in all our relationships, even when things are going well. Does it drift into the professional realm? Of course, it does. We could argue it is even more prevalent in the dynamics

discussed on these pages. Human nature is exacerbated when there is financial upside, or downside at stake for all parties.

Planning for the future of wealth and business is an essential aspect of your life's work. When you see the topics and the people on your calendar or your caller ID, how do you feel? Are you excited or resigned, curious, or distracted? Is there a sense of possibility and exploration, or the slow creep of dread, the walls of limitation closing in on you?

This premise is at the core of your quandary. If the relationship isn't as good as you'd like it to be, and the central subject of the relationship is big, the resulting friction is a persistent itch to a scab that won't heal on its own. Our psyche longs to preserve the connection, while our emotions and business acumen are distracted by lack of hope. Mutual parties convene to do great work, yet everyone is minding their Ps and Qs, poised in restraint against the relationship's true potential.

Professional courting and engagement are like adult dating. If you've observed a friend or family member thrust into it, you've probably noticed (perhaps painfully) that early attraction often fails to align with long-term sustainability. The things that attract two parties to each other at the beginning often lack the enduring qualities the relationship will need when it's no longer new and more often tested.

Anyone can bump into passion. In neuropsychologist Dr. Daniel Lieberman's book, *The Molecule of More*, he explained the difference between passionate love and companionate love. Passionate love is driven by dopamine and has a nine-month life cycle. From there, serotonin takes over and companionate love kicks in, less crackle and fire, more Duraflame. Our neurotransmitters are hard-wired toward these phases. What's the point? If you're entering a relationship with the hope of long-term sustainability, you have to vet for the companionate phase. The alternative? Nine months in, or sadly, later, you might hear Nancy Sinatra singing her 1965 hit song in the background, *These Boots Are Made for Walkin'*. You can't help wondering what was so enticing at the onset, or "What was I thinking?"

When two parties have the same wants and needs, you can play big in the mutual sandbox of possibility and clarity, high-quality outcomes, and easy adjustments. Hope becomes your ally – it no longer matters who is right or wrong – it's about celebrating the process of partnering. It turns out that when smart people who care about the same things come to the table excited to solve and create, the outcomes are far more effective.

Alignment and transparency decrease friction, yet they also mitigate surprises. Both sides lean in hard with their listening gears at full throttle. You are as interested in hearing the other person's vantage point as voicing your own. Being in a place of risk together creates the pathway to mutual wins. Might this expand the magnitude of the collective outcomes?

The Anatomy of an Unanticipated Event
Most unsavory surprises between affluent families and professional advisors fall into one of three sneak waves.

1. Could have been averted.
2. Outside the field of view – yours, theirs, or the collective.
3. Outside of all parties' control.

If all parties to the relationship sit still long enough on the front-end of relational and technical vetting, and fully show up in the relationship over time, the probability of being smacked from behind by one of the first two sneak waves noted above dramatically decreases.

When number three hits, you are ideally situated to see the full landscape with ease. Egos were long since checked at the door. And, because of prior partnering and the presence of Verified Data, you have access to a full set of options, not a limited or partial set. You are pre-wired for swift and ideal action. Your relational payoff is an exponentially stronger outcome than a limited relationship could ever produce.

The Magic and Nuance of Partnering
Pause for a moment and give yourself the gift of curiosity. Are your important relationships strong enough to invite relational candor, not only technical candor? If not, what is the ripple effect of that partial reality?

It's easy to make a dangerous assumption that everyone in business has an authentic desire to partner. Sadly, collaboration has taken on such lip service that we can no longer trust the language. If you want to test someone's collaborative claims, ask them to share an example – something that came up in their life, personally or professionally in the past few weeks, and how they partnered to a better outcome. If they go wide-eyed with a blank stare, ask yourself, "How's that working for you?"

Misalignment's three claims to fame are abdication, complacency, and blame.

Lack of partnering is often co-dependent. There is abdication in both directions. Families don't have the inclination or bandwidth to go deep into the technical territory. Advisors are flattered by the you-choose-I-trust-you dynamic. The payoff in ego or compensation can stoke the fires of superficial interaction on big important issues. If you abdicate or allow abdication, you are a co-conspirator to the outcome.

Complacency is the antithesis of stewardship. When you are an active steward of your relationships – and the decisions made inside of the relationships – you will achieve better results. We must teach ourselves to spot friction and stay one step ahead of its festering – to work through it together – before it's no longer solvable.

Blame is another common trigger that blocks deep partnering. Consider Eric Clapton's song, Before You Accuse Me. When something takes you by surprise, ask yourself what each party contributed to the blindsiding. If one or both of you weren't fully partnering prior to the surprise, you've got the olive branch of inquiry to mitigate recurrence.

Jack and Dena Morehouse
"We founded our company in 1998. We had $600 between us. I opened my laptop and said, 'We could be a consulting company... we can do better at this survey thing.' We had a lot of lean years. We were very much middle class.

We started with just me and my partner Dave, then there were five employees (now there are 350). My partner Dave and I designed and created an online survey platform. Our partners handled operations, programming, and sales. Dena came alongside as our office manager. Somewhere around 2001, Joe reached out and hired us to help him design a survey for one of their companies, The Founders Group. It was a business owner assessment around what founders of companies might be struggling with. Little did we know we would become Joe's client 18 years later.

Fast forward to 2019. Out of the blue, we got that call that you always hear about other business owners getting. Some venture capitalists connected with us and said, we want to buy controlling interest of the company and we want to buy it now. We soon learned that there was quite a bit of interest for a company with no debt, 97 percent client retention, and nearly zero employee turnover. We were skeptical, but they convinced us they could move Perceptyx along faster than we could.

So, I called Joe. He and I had kept in touch as friends over the years and more than being smart, we liked him and felt safe with them – Joe, Steve, Alex Matuk, and the team. We had done well financially before the sale, but not like this. It was all brand-new territory. You have to be able to talk to someone who is familiar with these things because suddenly you realize that none of your experiences could prepare you for what to do with the significant capital gained by the sale.

We felt an obligation to do right by the opportunity and not end up squandering the proceeds to taxes or mismanaging and losing it all. So, we sat down with Joe and started talking and it went from there.

They walked us through everything from a tax perspective, an investment perspective, and a giving perspective. But their main questions weren't actually financial. They wanted to learn what we like doing in life and family, where did we see ourselves, and what did we think we wanted to do with the proceeds from the sale. From the beginning, they helped us to keep focused on what was important. They converted that into viable options and strategies.

They always said that any strategy is only as good as its congruence with your goals. They helped us have clarity about what we wanted from the sale for ourselves and our family. It was like the Lewis Carroll quote, 'If you don't know where you are going, any road will get you there.'

We have always felt like Joe and their teams were very family oriented. Family was the number one core value in our company, so it just felt right. I don't think we knew at the time how much we were going to need their help and protection.

We had never thought a lot about estate planning or any of that. We didn't know a lot of the details. And we are still learning all the time and things are changing all the time, so you need advisors who get you and stick by you, looking out for you in ways that you don't know to look for. Most importantly, help from smart people that you can only trust.

When we started to navigate the sale, we didn't think we were going to need a lot of help because we had a very friendly relationship between the partners. But the deeper we went into it, we realized the larger issue was how to manage the sudden increase in liquid assets. Had it not been for Joe and Steve, I'm pretty sure we would not have gotten through it correctly.

We hadn't worked with many outside advisors at the time, but we knew we wanted people who would really get us. They needed to be smart but that wasn't the most important factor.

Financial recommendations didn't mean that much to us. Even walking into their office that first time, we were looking at some of the things they had on the wall, and it felt very much like our own company.

That alignment made it possible for them to create financial strategies that were wildly successful for us. You can move mountains when you have positive alignment around goals and mission, and you can't do anything without positive alignment around those things.

So many wealth management people behave in certain ways because it's how they make their money. They talk the talk, but they don't walk the walk. You have to put the time in to really get to know the people you are going to trust with your family, not just for us but for our kids and grandkids. Be cautious. Trust but verify. Get referrals from people who you know and trust. Find people who believe that people are more important than money.

If we had to share our wisdom with other families about this journey, we would say it is important not to wait. It is easy to put it off, raising a family, running a business. But you never know when you are going to get that call and being prepared for it matters."

A We-Driven Mindset

We define partnering as a We-Driven Mindset. There is a spirit of celebration around the pursuit of an outcome, not an answer. When a question arises outside of the collective wheelhouse, there is safety in the vulnerability of a proactive admission, "I don't know, but we can find out." This cabinet of adversaries is grounded in the shared knowledge that healthy discord and debate produce deeper thinking – amalgamated outcomes that no one-dimensional expert or contributing party could produce alone.

Please remember that this journey is not about firing each other. It's about peeling back the layers of what is working and what is not working. With awareness, we become curious. We hold hope for fixing what is broken, knowing that repairing a longstanding relationship is often less arduous than forging out into the unknown of new suitors. We look first for what can be true, even where it isn't obvious already. Is it ever too late to re-evaluate and help each other adjust? Isn't this part and parcel of any important relationship?

When you have a question about your financial, legal, or tax affairs, what is your first inclination? Do you action it yourself, or push it aside lacking the personal bandwidth and outside resources to address it? Or do you dial someone you trust who will answer on the first ring? Or find the additional talent via referral from your trusted, longstanding team?

Honor the Elephants
After more than 25 years of coaching and counseling affluent families, we know from experience that radical insight comes from a willingness to:

- look up from the status quo;
- question yourself, and other people, in search of new truths, not verification that you've been right all along;
- confront the brutal facts;
- seek understanding and clarity; and
- take decisive action.

This journey is not about creating wholesale chaos in your advisory relationships. Yet, if you sense they are not all love and rockets, bite off a piece of the elephant that is in the proverbial room. Do it in private, so you never have to tell anyone what you discover. Step into curiosity with solidarity, knowing that if you've ever felt exhausted or frustrated, you are not alone. In fact, it's likely that all of your peers have had the same exhale of stress into the wee hours of a sleepless night.

Clarity offers up power and control on the silver platter called choice. If, or when, you decide to make a change, you'll know exactly what you are looking for and why, and how to discern when you've found it.

Confront the Brutal Facts
Jim Collin's book, *Good to Great*, revealed that the great companies had a systemic drive to confront the brutal facts. Wealth is a business like any other. Improvement begins with an authentic search for the truth of what is either broken, or suffering in mediocrity.

You have a ninja-like skill for asking great questions and seeing the answers through a different or more distant lens. Yet, something in our society has taught you to suppress your survival sensors in this crucial domain. It's time to reclaim your toolbox.

The Elements of Alignment: Know Your Octopus
- Technical expertise including main lanes and specialties within specialties.
- Compensation models of the advisory firms including financial incentives, biases, and professional licenses.
- Commitment to bring your full self to the relationship, equipped with candor, and curiosity.

- Demographic clarity about who you can best serve, and who can best serve you.
- Life stages and events (the family's and the advisor's).
- Communication styles.
- Coping mechanisms.
- Billable hours and bandwidth.

Technical excellence is table stakes in planning for affluent families. Every advisory firm has what we refer to as lanes in particular areas of expertise and focus. Partners within the firm may specialize in distinct areas, or the whole firm may work in a particular deep dive of talent in one primary area.

For families, life with wealth is the widest, multi-lane freeway on the planet. Needs are vast and diverse with constant interchanges and overpasses in constant flux.

For advisory firms, every lane poses a choice, to learn it, hire it, buy it, or partner it. Each of these choices begs for authenticity. If a firm decides to learn a new lane, or hire talent into the firm, how deep and thorough is their expertise? Is it commensurate with the level of depth the family requires to achieve optimal technical outcomes? If not, who is proactively raising the additional needs to the family's radar? Does the threat of wallet-share influence the advisors' proactivity to partner with outside colleagues?

The journey to alignment begins by reverse engineering your present experience. When your criteria becomes a clear, active filter, it frees everyone up to fully partner.

Often the most accessible starting point is the reversal of negatives. If we can look to what is uncomfortable - a prior bad outcome, or less than ideal - we can seek to convert the status quo to a hope chest of positive aspirations.

If each party understands their own needs, capabilities, and expectations, and that of the other, there is no grey area or guessing. Imagine a planning meeting at which everyone knows why their tablemates chose to be at the table, how they were chosen to be there, and how or why, they are still there.

THE RELATIONSHIP T-SHEET AWARENESS EXERCISE

Grab a notebook and make three columns. For families, the left-hand column is a list of everyone who touches your wealth (financial, legal, tax, real estate, business advisors). For advisors, it is a list of your top 20 client families. In the next two columns, unpack your status quo, and aspire to those private alternatives. Below is an example.

FAMILY'S RELATIONSHIP T-SHEET		
Name (individual, firm)	**How things have always been**	**Permission to question**
Alex, the Attorney	Super smart, yet I often don't understand the problem or the recommendations.	All my life I've been an exceptionally strong problem-solver. I'd like to feel included in the whys and hows.
Ivan, the Investment Advisor	He's an A+ player, who lends cachet and confidence.	What is the definition of an A+ player? Is it my definition, my buddy's, or someone else's with different asset levels and priorities?
Sally, the Certified Public Accountant	Gratitude to her and her firm for that once-a-year blood bath on my personal and business tax filings.	Their firm can't possibly stand in the shoes of my wealth. If I was more engaged, what would I discover and how much would I save?

ADVISOR'S RELATIONSHIP T-SHEET		
Name **(individual, family)**	**How things have** **always been**	**Permission** **to question**
Evan, the Engineer	We suffer through the additional modeling and the incessant skepticism.	Maybe we can discuss his learning style, and what he craves to make a confident decision. Or maybe, there is a different path to feeding his needs that works for both of us.
Neil, the "Never-Has-Time"	We have a thirty-minute window and it's often cancelled at the last minute. My team preps and re-preps the same minutia. It's exhausting for all of us.	Perhaps we can share the commitment we have made to the relationship, and what our teams are doing behind the scenes. This may allow him to see the impact of his actions on our firm and see if he cares.
The Three-Generation Gyroscope	We want to be more directly impactful with the second and third generations. However, families often won't let us get that close, and we feel powerless.	Maybe we can set a specific conversation to explain why this work matters, and how we might partner with the family to preserve their long-term connectivity as a family. If we are not comfortable raising the topic, who will?

REVERSING THE DOMINOES
AWARENESS EXERCISE

When something big catches you by surprise in your advisory relationships, how do you react? Reach outside your perspective and anticipate what other people were thinking, or doing, and why. Seek revelation before judgment. For this exercise, imagine a complex domino formation, and imagine you are viewing the matrix from above. Notice the last domino that fell hard, and identify the dominos that preceded it, yet are less visible in the heat of the moment. To do so, ask yourself the following questions and record your insights in your notebook.

- Was it an innocent mistake that is unlikely to recur?
- Were there external influences outside of your collective control (the markets, economy, change in laws)?
- Was there a missing skillset that could have prevented the surprise?
- Was there a misalignment of expectations around the topic or project?
- Was there poor behavior from one or more parties? If so, what were they trying to advance or protect? What did they stand to lose or gain?
- Was I asleep at the wheel?

Take your notes from the above questions and parse them into the chronology that led to the last falling domino. Importantly, work from the right side of the grid backward, as below, starting with domino number 5. Record your observations in the *What happened?* row, as below.

Next, resketch the scenario from a positive perspective.

Working from left to right, design domino 1 to your ideal, then 2, and so forth. Consider the questions below as support for your brainstorming, and record your observations in the *How could it be better?* row, as below.

- How fixable is the relationship dynamic?
- How interested are you in fixing it?
- Who can help?
- Are the technical talents present?

	Domino 1	Domino 2	Domino 3	Domino 4	Domino 5
What happened?					
How could it be better?					

Give yourself a hug. Life, wealth, and relationships are all about cause and effect. No outcome exists in a vacuum of relational influences. It is most likely that the last domino was preceded by a misunderstanding of facts or motives, from the original choosing and being chosen relationship dynamics. Invite curiosity and self-compassion to be your allies in contemplation.

With your increased awareness, you can now contemplate what – if anything – you'd like to do with the information. Is it possible to upgrade your incumbent relationships from neutral to joyful? Are you equipped to have the dialogue on your own, or would external facilitation buffer the risks and the downsides? Are there new or additional players who can supplement your team to round out the rough edges or missing nuggets of contribution?

Once again, give yourself permission to answer these questions in private. Let them re-spark your natural joy for discernment and problem solving. Remember who you are, your strengths, and all that got you here. "You've got this."

Chapter 3

Built to Partner

Indulge me for a moment while we traverse some of your major milestones in life and business. Think of the best hire you have ever made. How much self-honesty did you pour into the decision? Through your decades of entrepreneurship, how much time and wisdom have you invested in mentoring your key people? How long did you court your spouse before saying Yes to yourself and the world?

Recall a proud parenting moment, a poignant pause that led to a win. How many hours did you spend teaching your first child to ride a bike? How many falls did you prevail over together, before that final wobbly glide into the freedom of two-wheel bliss?

What would these relationships be like without your soul-deep involvement in the bricks and mortar of those seminal journeys? Human beings are innately built to partner. We value connection with our cherished relationships. Fear of losing connection is a constant, even when we are not actively thinking about it.

Now, consider the things you cherish most in life, health, family, inner circle relationships, and your business. Wealth allows you to support, protect, and celebrate these anchors. Your advisors help you optimize and protect your wealth. Does anyone see where I'm going here?

Create a mental list of your top three to five financial, legal, insurance, and tax advisors. How much courting and vetting went into the pre-engagement-get-acquainted phase of the journeys? During your tenure together, how often have you allocated an entire meeting to a relational check-in and tune-up?

In our experience, successful families and business owners allocate an average of two hours to pre-learning their key professional advisors before agreeing to what each party espouses to be a long-term relationship. A portion of that time is often a casual conversation during golf or cocktails. Doused in subjectivity and leaning into engagement, you give the new tribe member the keys to your kingdom before you can spell their last name.

Thinking big about things that matter immensely is intellectually exhausting, especially when there is no clear path to a successful outcome on the far side of effort. Choosing your advisory tribe is one of those big things. Families long to absolve the pain of the search, do a good job, and make it go away for a while. Technical complexity exponentializes the challenge. You can't possibly know if their claims and solutions are true, or if they are right for you. The leap of faith is the largest Band-Aid you'll ever remove. Who wouldn't seek a swift rip?

Why don't we vet?
- *Lack of methodology to create a selection criteria.*
- *Lack of methodology to activate the criteria as a filter.*
- *Lack of transparency around the cost-benefit trade-offs of your options, emotionally and financially.*
- *The perception that as long as they are smart, or kind, the rest doesn't matter.*

- *The sense that additional effort will fail to produce a meaningfully different result.*

In addition to pain and complexity, we believe there are two key reasons successful families and business owners may not thoroughly vet prospective advisors. Side note, if you are thinking, "That's not me" please stay with the premise for a few minutes.

First, perhaps you did vet someone thoroughly in the past and even with all the tire-kicking, their unsavory traits were kept expertly out of sight until after the hire. Once revealed, you were so far in, it was tough to discern which was worse – sticking with the wrong choice – or reversing your car over the parking lot's No Exit tire shredder to begin again.

Second, neither families nor firms have a process or protocol for proper due diligence. Ironically, it is the advisors themselves – as long as they genuinely care about right-fit relationships – who are best suited to design your vetting protocol. Next time you meet an advisor you respect yet don't plan to hire, ask this question, "If you were coaching yourself about how to discern a right-fit advisory relationship, what are the top three to five tough questions you'd ask?"

In the meantime, we will share our own inside scoop. We hope you'll select what resonates and create a personal protocol.

Comparing and contrasting potential resources and people to objectively discern their potential fit for you, your family, your business, and key people.

Note that we intentionally put 'you' first in the list because, as a servant leader, you are likely to put your needs last much of the time. In this realm, it is important to put yourself and your spouse first.

If all goes well with your vetting, you and your advisors will be partnering to protect your family, business, and key people and assets. Liking and enjoying your advisors (and them liking you) is inextricably linked to the quality of the work you will do and the results you will achieve – both technically and relationally – in good times and bad.

Flawed from the Start: Common Blind Spots Around Timing, Time Horizon, and Criteria

Many people associate vetting with the pre-launch of a thing, a prospective relationship with a concept, idea, or person. Either you have a solution and you are looking for an expert to implement it, or you have an idea and you are looking for methodologies to execute it.

With an immediate need or an imminent transaction, there is legal, financial, or tax work to be done. Vetting defaults to the here and now, inadvertently limiting your outcome. Too often, you will wind up with an advisor who knows how to solve the predefined problem in a specific way, just like they have solved it for others who don't share your fact pattern, time horizon, or financial makeup. At the risk of offering a painful analogy, if you go to a dental root canal specialist, you will receive a great root canal. If you consult a periodontist, you might discover some additional choices.

Imagine a highly appreciated piece of real estate. You can sell it with an eye toward minimizing the tax consequences, yet tax is only one factor. What is your long-term goal for this bucket of wealth? How does it serve you or others currently, and how could it serve in the future? Does it diversify your risk by maintaining wealth outside the business? Could it augment a family member's future income, or provide a management role for an adult heir? If you do sell, what happens when the asset class shifts from illiquid to liquid? Sure, you can hand the post-transaction check to your investment advisor. However, vetting for long-term vision at the onset raises your innate strategic antennae. It may lead you to an advisor with a broader lens and possibly a deeper toolbox, someone who may expand and integrate your choices.

Importantly, families can adjust the vetting depth based on magnitude and time horizon. If the outcome goes south, how long will it stay with you emotionally, financially, and relationally? If you are vetting a private cruise that will be completed in two weeks, the risk is fairly low, unless it's the final voyage you will make with an aging parent.

From a criteria perspective, at your early interactions, take a pause to notice whether the prospective advisor communicates in a manner you can get your arms around. Even with highly technical topics, you've earned the right to be selective regarding communication style. If you feel like your head is going to explode and you haven't even dug into the big stuff, talk to a few more people. Give yourself permission to be a student of the early experience.

Here is a great litmus test. If you feel like you are receiving a long, convoluted explanation to a straightforward question, the advisor might not have the purported depth of expertise or perceived experience. Lengthy dialogue can be a cover for a weak argument, self-motivation, or short-term gain. Further, they should be able to explain the upside and downside with equal vigor, as well as how they actively monitor the integrity of the strategy throughout its decades-long life cycle. Planning is never a one-and-done event.

Relational Right-Fits

If technical expertise is an advisor's ticket into the stadium, relational fit is their ticket onto your playing field. Families make a valiant effort to evaluate perceived technical prowess, yet relational fit is an afterthought, rarely considering baseline enjoyment of each other's company as a relevant metric. Ironically, most families are better equipped to judge character and camaraderie than a technical subject that requires degrees and decades to master.

Your pre-vetting pool of candidates must begin with professionals who are highly referred, upper echelon, top performers. Yet from that pool, relational vetting should come first. Allow your innate wisdom to renavigate your first meetings. Do you feel relaxed and heard, with conversation flowing easily? Are you at the mercy of a prebound pitch book, with a cuff around what you can ask, and when? If you were explaining something complex to someone who had little or no orientation to the topic, would you treat the person the way you are currently being treated?

Notice the advisor's advice-bias. Is their firm in growth mode, or is it shrinking due to market pressures? What financial incentives underpin their purported best practices?

Do they have a new skill, capability, product, or practice area that is driving them? What other seen or unseen personal, familial, or professional influences are in the room with you?

As you embark on this process, remember that it's not about eliminating imperfect outcomes. The reality is that even with strong vetting, savvy people get duped sometimes. Process and protocol will increase your discernment and objectivity. Select the best of the best from the referred pool – or be willing to eliminate everyone in front of you – and revisit your search from scratch. Vetting reminds us that sometimes you have to slow down to move fast.

HEAR FROM JOE: AUDIO OVERVIEW #4

Simple Ways to Shift
Begin with a pool of candidates who are purported to have the technical depth you require. Then, vet first for relational fits. Apply your innate intellectual rigor. Remind yourself not to let current exhaustion over the choosing, or prior experience of being chosen, cloud your discernment.

Who makes the cut?
- *People I'm drawn to spend time with.*
- *People I can easily communicate with.*
- *People I'd send my kids to for advice.*

Perhaps you are thinking this is counterintuitive. Obviously, engaging the smartest or most experienced advisor on the list will result in better outcomes. Or will it?

When two people are drawn to be in a relationship, everyone's walls come down. Safety invites your own clarity to take a significantly deeper dive. It invites the advisors' technical potential to reach equal depth. Each of you is more interested in hearing the other person's viewpoint than your own. Listening deepens for everyone at the table. Collaborative innovation reveals new and otherwise undiscoverable truths. Sounds pretty outcome-driven to me.

After the relational first-cut, vet for technical excellence, and technical right-fits. Importantly, these are two vastly different criteria. Default vetting is too often focused on the short-term. Pick a smart person to execute the thing or transaction that is directly in front of you. Candidates are prematurely narrowed, right fit, right now.

Instead, vet for the long-term outcome for which you aspire. What benefit are you hoping to achieve, not from the transaction but from the asset, action, or decision? What will success look like 10, 20, 30 years out? Reducing tax or shielding an asset is not a benefit. A benefit is the ultimate purpose and outcome of the action you are taking currently.

Create Your Vetting Toolbox and Make it Your Reliable Friend

Vetting is inherently a partnering behavior. Through personal interviews and external reference checks are step one on the journey away from abdicating and into partnering.

Begin your interviews by asking about a scenario in the last month – either a problem or an opportunity – that required partnering. How did they participate or collaborate? When other parties were reticent to partner towards a solution or own an outcome, how did they invite a shared experience to the table to benefit the family?

Next, ask the prospective advisor to describe their belief system and behavior for when things go wrong. Listen through a filter of your gut instinct. If this person made a mistake, would they wait for you to discover it, or come proactively to the table with candor, accountability, and protocol?

Request specific historic examples. General responses are a masterful distraction when a person is unable or unwilling to go deep.

- Tell me about a time when something went terribly wrong.
- Who discovered it, and how was it discovered?
- How was it dealt with, or remedied?

Attune your antennae as much to their affect as to their actual response. Lean into your own discomfort. If you are hesitant to ask something, there is likely data on the far side of the question that will protect you from future grief.

Next, paint the picture of the pain point or project you wish to address, including the long-term benefit to which you aspire. When they hone in on a particular methodology, ask about alternative ways to achieve your stated benefit, including some that are outside of their internal wheelhouse. If the way they know is described as the only way to go, interview more advisors.

Importantly, take care not to ask a specialist to vet a holistic game plan. They may lack the broad perspective, or the personal incentive, to recommend a solution outside the walls of their firm.

Deep reference checks can be a major abdication blind spot. We all know we should conduct them prior to aligning with long-term partners, but it's so much easier to move toward Yes than to discover why the answer might be No. Except that it's not. Consider the use of your most precious resources, time, energy, intellectual bandwidth – yours, your family's, your teams – and the raw financial factors. Isn't it less depleting in all of these areas to choose carefully at the onset, than to live with a less-than-ideal choice, or re-choose in the future?

Build your vetting muscle memory by asking to speak specifically to the families whose examples were shared by the advisor. Create a safe environment for the families' candor. No advisory relationship is perfect. Push into the pregnant pauses. Here too, generalities are smooth spackle for cracks they prefer not to reveal. Pose the same questions to each of the families with whom you speak. Look for consistencies and discrepancies. Take the discrepancies back to the advisor and unpack them together.

Here are specific questions to play with:

- Tell me about a time when they had your back in an area you wouldn't have noticed on your own.
- When you ask them to do something they disagree with, do they comply, or push back with deeper questions?
- How do they treat their own colleagues and team members while they are in the room, and equally important, when they are not in the room?
- Are they more likely to own a problem, or throw someone else under the bus?

- How do they show up with your spouse and family members, and your key people in the business? Is there equal commitment to those relationships or are they treated as obligatory favors?
- How do they reply when they don't know the answer to a question from you or your other advisors?
- What are their follow up processes for year two and beyond of an executed strategy or decision?

Bill & Tina Howe

"Bill and I had built and run the business together for decades. Over time, our three girls had chosen to come and work with us. Each of them took the initiative to secure a license or certification that was critical to growing the company. They're all very hard workers, not entitled. Each of them really earned their role in the business.

We had a significant issue with one of our daughters. It literally tore our family apart. We had lost our family harmony, fighting and finger pointing, and we could've lost a division of the business. In desperation, and maybe hope too, I Googled "family coaches". Surprisingly, I didn't find much but I did find Carmen Bianchi who appeared to be quite well regarded. Bill and I got together with her, and it turned out she wasn't taking on new clients, but she highly recommended Joe and his team.

So, all five of us got together with Joe to see if he could help us and if we would be a good fit. We came out of that meeting feeling like we could make it. We had a whole weekend with him, all five of us. He took us down to our core, talking to the girls about how they grew up, how they saw us as parents, what had affected them. In every family, each child has a different personality, and he saw behind their curtains.

Prior to all this, Bill and I found ourselves getting stuck, because we didn't want to splinter our family. Joe allowed the girls to speak freely to us as their parents, so we could understand truly how they felt about the business, their strengths, their weaknesses. There were a lot of tears, yet a lot of learning too. I saw some things I wasn't aware of about myself. I was micromanaging the girls; they couldn't do anything right.

Joe often says, "Hope is a great conversation." The hope came during that weekend. We started that Friday at a very low point. He took us through all these exercises, and those helped us talk everything through. That's when we knew that we were going to be okay. We were going to get through this. We were going to thrive and it was going to be even better than it had been before all the hurt.

The weekend was hard, but it truly allowed us to take a step back and see things that mattered. They're going to win or they're going to fail. But either way, they have to go through it on their own in order to learn. Like most parents, we have a great love for our children, and we'll do anything for them. We were very close before. We just lost our footing for a while and Joe helped us get it back.

As parents in business together with your kids, and other family members, it's tough. Some will become the cream that rises to the critical top, and some won't. You have to find a coach who can help you sort through the business side of that objectively yet be sensitive to how to communicate and execute decisions which are not always popular.

You've got to take your time to find the right counseling fit. You can't rush it. We interviewed several people and the others were *professional, but they were focused on what they wanted to do, not what our core issues were. You have to do the research and keep in mind what's at stake.*

For me, it was my girls. I love them deeply. They've always been my everything. I did everything I possibly could to keep the family unit together. I didn't care if they worked in the business. It wasn't important, but I didn't want to lose them. Now the girls have successfully taken over the business and we couldn't be more proud.

At the end of the day, the work is really for the kids, not for you as parents. It's for their next stage in their life. They need direction. You can tell a child something forever. They're not going to listen most of the time. So having a third party is what can get everybody unstuck, individually and together.

Within a few months of working with Joe, we could see that the girls were aligning again. We've always been such a good family but we needed help getting back to that. Sometimes we talk to friends who have family issues or family business issues and they don't want to open the can of worms, but you have to. You can't let it all slip away out of fear of dealing with the hard realities.

Anyone in a family business knows that it's not all about money. We knew we needed to work with someone that understands the unique dynamics of a family business, and frankly someone who would take the time to understand us as parents.

We're in the plumbing business so it's the same as teaching one of our plumbers how to go into someone's home and have them feel safe about it. Nobody wants a plumber to come to your door.

*In our company, when we have new plumbers join our team,
they say they've never worked in a company where the customer
was happy to see us. So that's what the right coach can do for
your family."*

Vetting for Highly Technical Expertise

The journey of vetting for technical expertise advisors is at
best a magical mystery tour, much like figuring out how to
parent your first kid or hire a key person in your business.
Perfection is an unlikely outcome. Throughout your life,
you have – on purpose or accidentally – found technical
expertise that can check the boxes. What got you here may
not have enough fire power for the current magnitude and
complexity of your wealth and family. In this expanded
realm, there is no magical way to prevent disasters or
predict conflict. The approach we are describing makes an
imperfect journey less taxing, more effective, and ultimately,
even joyful.

So many of the families we meet left their innate
discernment skills along the roadside of advisory choices
a long time ago. Sometime in the past, you did the good
work of vetting and still, disaster and friction prevailed. If
we could turn back the clock, we might notice that all great
intentions were in play. However, the skills noted below may
have been muzzled in hopes of putting the pain of choosing
behind you.

As you create and implement your personal vetting
protocol, take care not to acquiesce the instincts that have
prevailed through life's unknowns in business, parenting,
and difficult economic times. Invite your skills to reclaim
their seat at your table and become your advisory board. It

wasn't the act of vetting that disserved you, it was the lack of process and protocol for vetting thoroughly.

Following are the top seven innate skills we observe in successful families and business owners:

1. Too-good-to-be-true
When your risk or reward alarm bings its trusty signal, you are naturally inclined to the pause of caution. Is the person or opportunity at hand a really good thing, or too-good-to-be-true? You invite deeper exploration – rather than shy away from it – and typically with more than one source. You verify your hypotheses with questions, in search of opposing viewpoints, not the easier route of confirming your own.

2. Blanket trust versus conditional trust
You naturally discern how deep and wide to trust in particular scenarios and relationships, even when total trust is the easier default. Others abdicate blanket trust – the wholesale belief that another party will never put their interest above yours. You favor conditional trust as a healthy bias at the beginning of a relationship, knowing that any individual may have a financial incentive, a knowledge set bias, or the inclination to advocate or defend a peer.

3. Experience becomes wisdom
Through bionic observation of situations, events, and behaviors – in your personal experiences and hearing of others' – you notice both the cause and effect of the myriad scenarios. Where others lament outcomes, you have x-ray vision for the initial catalysts, cataloguing the data points to pre-empt future messes.

4. Sense of good people

You have an uncanny aperture for spotting authenticity – folks with a proverbial good head on their shoulders – during the early stage of getting acquainted. You know when you don't want to stay in conversation or spend time with the person or group in the future. You're willing to disconnect from someone, especially when the stakes are low. Ironically, it can be harder to disconnect when the stakes are higher.

5. The far side of honesty

You can sense if someone will do the right thing when no one's watching. You have x-ray vision for their internal barometer of, "Is it right, it is wrong, or will I get caught?" regardless of whether it's a $5.00 bill or a $50K blunder. And, you remain curious for evidence that will confirm or deny your hunch.

6. Uncommon connection

You have a heightened ability to initiate and establish connections with people, and to notice when the outreach falls flat, or is met with disingenuous behavior. You are a natural and skilled observer of how people show up and treat others in their tribe or community. Your antennae are equally accurate when you are directly involved, or observing from the outside looking in.

7. Common sense

Does the person, opinion, or recommendation make common sense? You refuse to relinquish your caution flag, instead staying the course to ask follow-up questions, validating, or disproving the data and your hypotheses.

Perhaps the best thing about grounding back to your own wisdom is that you don't have to actually do anything, except get out of your own way. I recognize this might sound harsh, yet in truth, it is a mirror to your daily reality. You are out there every day helping people be their best selves. It's the hero's journey of servant leadership. The seven skills described above are simply the elixir of your own offered back to you.

Whatever your shortlist of the seven, perhaps augmented by some we haven't thought of, you can show up willing and ready, with the courage to deploy them. The stakes are high. You are in these advisory relationships to protect your most important personal and entrepreneurial relationships. When everyone brings their superpowers into the room, there is a sense of fully processing each other, both technically and relationally. Curiosity invites the counterpunch of relevant questions, questions that further your clarity, others' clarity, and the collective.

The laws of learning agility make it cumulative, allowing you to consistently strengthen your foundation. New topics are met with the joy and ease of knowing, not where you are going, but what you have the power and potential to achieve. It's a place of finding the best answers together. Are you ready to take the risk?

"Trust but verify."
Ronald Reagan

The Simplicity of Self-Trust
Steve, my son Sal, and I, have been avid fly fishermen for

decades. We fish together in silence to release stress and heal our personal or professional wounds. We invite others to the water's edge, asking their permission to facilitate and mentor. We wade in deep, joyfully surrendering to the mentorship of our peers and younger generations.

In my early years of fly fishing, I never understood why, in a raging river, the current sometimes turns back on itself and goes still. My 'too-good-to-be-true sense' told me the water was defying physics. 'Experience becomes wisdom' invited me to look deeper. I learned that sometimes when water circles a big rock it becomes stagnant. I also learned that really big trout put out the least amount of effort possible to find food. It turns out food likes still water too, and once it enters the pool, it is trapped. My reward for applying innate discernment, regardless of place and circumstance? It forever changed the way I fly fish.

"Absolute power corrupts absolutely."
Lord Acton

Stewardship: The Practice of Continuous Vetting

Definition of Stewardship
Having the respect in a relationship to consciously check-in and adjust, proactively working to maintain a healthy and strong connection. The commitment to mutually assess and adjust for alignment, knowing that alignment is pure sympatico.

One of the most hazardous forms of abdication is the lack of intentional stewardship after the first year and into the future of an advisory relationship. Suffering in silence is a slippery slope. Relational measuring sticks are irrelevant and unfair if you're the only one who knows your success criteria.

Stewardship is quite simply the practice of continuous, intentional vetting throughout the life cycle of your important relationships. Consider when your car is out of alignment. You can drive it around in that state for months or years. Too late, you notice the tires are wearing unevenly. You go in for a realignment and drive off the lot astounded at the ease of motion. Instead of pushing the vehicle to perform, you're in partnership on the open road.

Early on in advisory relationships, everyone shows up doused in clarity about short-term needs and long-term strategic outcomes. Overtime, it's all too easy to slip into tactical mode. We run hard toward the wins and keep tight to the task lists. Time is currency and small talk is a ticking clock in search of an invoice. It's not that people are cold or unprofessional to each other, it's just that the work comes first.

We narrow the focus to an outcome, forgoing the pre-work necessary to nail the desired result. Your strategic endgame is changing all the time. That's why wealth and entrepreneurship are such a fun sandbox to play in. Life happens, putting internal and external pressure on family, business, and the relationships who support your thriving. This multi-faceted dynamic is the nucleus of the pre-work piece.

Stewardship is like having a great glass of wine with your own clarity. Sniff, swirl, and take that first sip of curiosity. Has the bottle aged well, or has time and circumstance let it go bad? Pause to ask yourself and your advisors, Do I still believe this? What outcome does it serve? Is that still what I want? Is it still the best I can do? Embrace the uncertainty of new truths that may self-reveal. Stewardship is tending as much to the quality of your relationships as the quality and completion of the work. Importantly, we must decorrelate gratitude from stewardship. Expressing a deep thank you and paying for an over-the-top dinner isn't the same as intentional curiosity about how you are doing together.

Stewardship is an alignment tune-up. It inclines people to take intellectual risks together. Risks are where the interesting dialogue resides. With mutual trust, the good stuff of relationship is more joyful, and navigating the messes and sneak waves is an Olympic grade team sport.

Buyer Beware: The Role of Conviction

Even the humblest of souls can be trapped by the lure of conviction, which narrows your aperture. We become so intent on getting the thing done, we stop looking for nuance or variables, ignoring the facts that don't fit our carefully constructed narrative.

Next time you head into a call or a meeting with an advisor, take a pause for a gut check. Are you involved in the moment, fully present in the dialogue? Or are you invested in your own preformed conclusion or inclination, or distracted by fee sensitivity, overwhelm, or boredom? Are you assessing to confirm your conviction, or to learn regardless? Are you unintentionally teeing everyone up to be yes-men, a request for complacency that conflicts with your desire for candor?

Remind yourself how much you enjoy being challenged. The thrill of debate with a cabinet of adversaries who are your intellectual peers. Recall the unexpected reveal of fresh thinking that's born of alternative perspectives.

Early in my first career, my mentor and boss, Frank Braglin, imparted this life wisdom, "It is in your success that you will find failure." This cold splash of water was accompanied by a gift, a laminated wood plaque with the definition of the word 'complacency'. Frank was a wise man, and his teaching was painful for my young ego.

We naturally conduct forensic post-mortems when there's a mistake, misstep, or misunderstanding, yet we forget to dig into the win's equal vigor. We let relational success become a callous to relational learning. Unpacking your greatest wins with your most important advisors isn't an ego trip, it's like watching game footage of the final plays that nailed the win: press pause, slow things down, and become an outside observer. Notice the nuance and variables. Let them be mentors, partnering in your next magical outcome.

Let Stewardship Lighten Your Load
Families abdicate stewardship because it feels hard and heavy. It's so much easier to focus on the technical aspects of strategy and solution. Working on the relationship feels like slowing down when you really need to go fast.

Bear with me, and please trust that these next thoughts are not a judgment of anyone personally. They are the composite of decades of observation, teaching, and counseling with families and advisors.

So, here goes. Abdication is your wingman for attracting disaster. It breeds misalignment, and mail-it-in recommendations. The void of stewardship habits and protocol prevents partnering.

If you don't prioritize pause, what does it tell your advisors about how they should show up? Lack of stewardship is like

reverse mentorship, inadvertently modeling the behavior
you least desire from others. It's an invisible Petri dish of
atrophy, discontentment, and malaise.

Fortunately, there is a Ying to the Yang. If you have done
the good work of vetting for relational fits, you enjoy
spending time with your advisors. Begin with the end in
mind. If you want the whole person to show up for you, let
the whole person be in the relationship. Learn the human
side of your advisory relationships. Know what is happening
in the lives, brains, hearts, and souls of the people across
the table.

Instead of asking how someone is doing out of courtesy
or obligation, align your inquiry with the importance of
the topics at hand. Ask meaningful, authentic questions.
Remember their details the way they remember yours.
This is not the time-suck of small talk, it is gaining
tacit awareness of what is in the room, affecting the
work anyway. Unspoken realities create distractions.
Compassionate inquiry dissipates the harsh edges, creating
safety in vulnerability. It lets the people you need to trust
feel trustworthy. Their ability to be real and raw without
reaction or judgment allows everyone's attention and energy
to funnel to the work.

Another harsh reality is that families and advisors don't
always show up prepared. When one side consistently
abdicates preparation, it gives the other side a duplicate
permission slip, you take the pink copy and give them the
yellow one.

For families, preparation isn't a To Do List, it's a mindset.
Certainly, you may need to review documents or statements,
but the technical review is far less important than preparing

yourself to be a fully present participant in your calls and meetings with your advisors. Consider the things in your life that create mental acuity: sleep, exercise, prayer, or meditation. Commit to these precursors the same way you would if you were running your company's board meeting or attending your kids' graduations and weddings. Instead of showing up to be reported to, come to the table with a learning mind.

- What might you discover that was unexpected?
- What isn't sitting right?
- What do you wish you could change?
- What validation or reinforcement is nourishing your instincts?

Your preparedness raises the bar for everyone in the room. Notice how on point your meetings become when you do the hard work of leading by example.

You now have a few morsels of fresh perspective to savor into a shift. Enjoy the exercises below, and as always, give yourself permission to do this work in private without the expectation of sharing it with anyone.

Adopt a Stewardship Mindset: A Five-Point Creed for Families and Their Advisors

While a shift to intentional stewardship can feel heavy or cumbersome at first, trust that it will transition to quantifiable impact on your planning outcomes and know that it will feel good too. Push through your resistance and be curious about thoughts you have tucked away from yourself or others, or that other people have guarded from you. Celebrate unknown factors and factor patterns. Use the following five-point creed as both touchstone and litmus test:

1. Celebrate new data, digest it, and be willing to change your position.
2. Enjoy the interactions, let optimism and engagement reveal new pathways.
3. Hear and experience other people's sharing: practice being acutely present.
4. Cultivate a genuine desire to understand other people's points of view without needing to agree, fix, or defend.
5. Create an environment (for yourself and other people) in which all participants can change their minds or shift their perspectives.

Use these questions to elicit reactions and be a student of the responses. Is the advisor defensive or stumbling, or are they contemplative and authentic? Importantly, advisors can pose these questions to families that they are considering engaging. Relational stewardship is, by definition, mutual and devoid of hierarchy.

1. Consider three regrets you have had in professional relationships in the past 90 days, little ones or big ones. What did you notice after the fact and what would you do differently next time?
2. Share a technical mistake that you or your firm made. How did it come to pass? When you realized it, what was your firm's process to deconstruct it, and implement new protocols?
3. In your best professional relationships, what results are you most proud of, and what do you bring to the process to intentionally foster them?
4. What do you tend to protect people from, that we should both be aware of, if we decide to work together?

RELATIONSHIP FILTER EXERCISE

Use this exercise to recall and unpack behaviors or patterns that have rubbed you the proverbial wrong way in current or past advisory relationships. Reference the table below for concrete examples. Once you have vented the negatives onto the page, convert them to aspirations to create your higher bar.

Behavioral Misfires: select a specific advisor or firm to contemplate. Recall as many moments as you can in which you noticed the other party behaving in a manner that sat uncomfortably outside of your core values. Perhaps they cancelled a meeting at the last minute, forgot to do an essential piece of research you requested, or chose not to own their behavior. Maybe they took more time than you'd like furtively defending a product or strategy, and you felt sold. Use the examples in the table below to stimulate your thinking. After you have completed the left-hand column proceed to the Relational Wins column. Importantly, discipline yourself to vent all of the misfires before moving into the positives.

Relational Wins: next, recall moments in which another person's character shone so brilliantly you almost reached for your sunglasses. Recall the choices that made you proud to be in relationship with them. Record your thoughts in the middle column of the table.

My Higher Bar: now you are ready for the fun stuff. Scan the first two columns for experiences that are opposite sides of the same behavioral coin. Convert them to flags of courage that you will plant in vetting for ideal fits, and for stewarding existing and long-term relationships.

Behavioral Misfires	Relational Wins	My Higher Bar
The answer to a question felt like a cover-up and it made me wonder what other cover-ups came before this one.	They noticed a fellow advisor's mistake and supported them in fixing it, instead of opportunistically throwing them under the bus.	Candor matters even when the content is painful or disruptive.
I felt like they were recommending and defending a strategy they designed for someone else without hearing my fact pattern uniquely.	They prioritized family over work that could wait another day without damaging an outcome.	Compassion prevails; humans make mistakes. We unpack them for future clarity not current blame.
They posed all the important questions directly to me, even though my spouse (and emotional rock) was sitting next to me.	They treated my assistant with genuine compassion and gratitude.	We treat each other and everyone else with equal kindness regardless of role and absent hierarchy.
	They made a technical mistake, yet they converted it to a positive.	We own our behavior and ask other people to be equally accountable.

My Higher Bar: A Stewardship Tool

As discussed, stewardship is simply the intentional practice of continuous vetting. As such, you can use your My Higher Bar bullets in year two and beyond, of your advisory relationships. Set aside a dedicated time and place solely for this conversation. Create an environment of celebration, not confrontation. Share a great bottle of wine or go for a walk and talk together. Print copies of My Higher Bar (yours, not ours). Review each point and discuss how you feel you are doing and your experience of the other person. Switch roles and hear the other person's perspective on both fronts. Open the dialogue to how you are doing together. Even if you feel out of alignment with the advisor at hand, make space for healthy, unguarded dialogue. Look for ways to mutually raise your relational bar.

Go deeper, using the open-ended stewardship questions below. Invite each party to contemplate and share regarding self and other.

- What were my initial goals for the planning or the relationship? Do I still have the same priorities and perspectives about the work? Was I candid at the beginning, and if not, what can I bring forth in the present to be helpful?
- What made us a good technical fit at the beginning? Are those factors still relevant? Have they expanded in such a way that we might augment our journey with external wisdom?
- What are you protecting me from that I should know?
- Have we grown together or outgrown each other?
- How did we do together when we faced a bad outcome?
- What has changed about my family, business, and myself? If we met each other today, how would I set the stage differently for our relationship?

INNATE SKILLS EXERCISE

Leverage the top seven innate skills described earlier in this chapter for a self-assessment about how you are showing up for your best professional relationships. List your advisors down the left side of the table, and the innate skills across the top. Add skills that we haven't thought of and remove any of ours that don't resonate. Rate yourself on a scale of 1 to 5, with 5 as the highest, regarding how fully and consistently, you are bringing the skill into the relationship.

Here's an example. When I meet with my attorney, I feel a little deflated. There is a level of intensity that syphons some of my attention span. In the hours and days that follow these meetings, I realize that I forgot to notice or articulate important factors or perspectives.

	Too-good-to-be true	Blank trust versus conditional trust	Experience becomes wisdom	Sense of good people	The far side of honesty	Uncommon connection	Common sense
Alex, the Attorney	5	4	3	2	5	3	4
Ivan, the Investment Advisor	5	3	5	4	2	2	2
Sally, the Certified Public Accountant	1	3	5	3	5	2	5

What matters most? After the heavy lifting from these exercises, sit quietly for a few minutes. Hold space for the correlation between effort and outcome. You have more agency and influence on these dynamics than the traditional, decades-long trajectory might tell you. Take a pause and pride yourself for cultivating your courage.

Chapter 4

The Four Phases
of Family Thriving

We approach this tender topic with a profound belief in families' potential to thrive. Matriarchs and patriarchs have a lifelong ache for their kids to do well. They long for their daughters and sons to experience the chest-puffing joy of a great choice, earn their own money, or impact a person or a cause. At times, that well-meaning message gets muffled, twisted, or misunderstood.

Those spaces between the ache of hope and the mishearing are the spaces of family counseling work. The Four Phases of Family Thriving – progress, hope, stewardship and governance – is the system through which a family can learn where they are currently, and how to design their path forward.

Parents, me included, are imperfect beings trying to master an elusive role. We navigate the family system in servant leadership, an other-first, self-second dance of what to do or say, and hope we notice when the anxiety of saying or doing nothing is the best mentorship of all.

The four-phase system guides a family from their current place on the continuum of angst – either mild relational friction and crunchiness, or outright pain – to a place of new or restored ease. Ease is often the precursor to finding your thriving. It creates openings for family alignment or Family Synergy Work, dramatically enhancing traditional family governance work.

Importantly, while we present the four-phase system as sequential, real life is anything but orderly. Families can use the cycle as a grounder to where they are, and where they aspire to journey. The phases are meant to serve regardless of chronology. Families often find themselves with a toe in multiple phases at the same time.

The cycle offers an intentional leveler to keep both faith and focus. It reminds us to be students of our potential when things get rough. Yet likewise, the cycle helps families go deeper when they are doing well, immersed in hope and curiosity, explorers on a mission to synergy.

In this chapter, we will look first at family governance – both the perceptions and definitions born of an industry – and the unspoken yet, just as real definitions that exist within every family system. We will navigate the progression from friction, or even at times toxicity, to the far side of healing, or what we call Family Synergy Work.

Through all of this, we rely on our trusty touchstones of curiosity and hope. Historic patterning from previous generations, or the current one, have the power to repeat themselves, yet only in the absence of those anchors. Whatever stress, aggravation, or anxiety you, the people you love, or your cherished assets are suffering from, please know in your heart that it doesn't have to be this way.

Governance

We begin by broadening the connotation of family governance – from an aspired cure-all endpoint – to the additional layers which are less often discussed and equally real. Governance is simply the correlation between intention and outcome. You can govern a community, its members, or a company. Governance establishes agreements for a healthy system of communication, behavior, and support. It sets forth hope that community members will act in certain ways. It offers a Plan B for when they don't, or for a time when the historic rule sets no longer serve the evolving system.

For successful families and businesses, governance is a set of rules that influence actions and reactions in the context of power and wealth. Long before a family hires governance advisors, brings in trustees, or establishes legal structures, governance is alive and well in the family system. These de facto dynamics, unspoken, and unwritten, are an Invisible Guest, sitting proudly at the intersection of expectation and outcome. What motives – yours or others, helpful or not helpful – are influencing your desire for traditional governance work?

Zia Sarafina's Homespun Approach

When my Aunt Sara, *Zia Sarafina*, made the voyage from Italy to America, a fresh-faced 16-year-old brought over the pond as a child bride to an older husband, she couldn't have fathomed the roles that respect, chocolate, and wealth would come to play in her family system. Sara and my uncle built their businesses together, and when he died in his 40s, she found herself with double the entrepreneurial complexity and three teenage boys to feed. She landed hard in the role of matriarch and held on tight for the remainder of her life. Meanwhile, the family made quick work of learning who had to pitch in for what, and the boys prevailed in their contributions to the family's wealth-building.

Along the way, the rules of the family system etched themselves deep in an invisible bench on which Aunt Sara perched her proprietary cushion. They went something like this. Bring chocolate. Make tea. Greet her with a kiss on the cheek, and at least five minutes of respect demonstrated by asking sincere questions. Respond to control with compliance.

Aunt Sara's style of governance suggested we learn the rules of the family system through osmosis. Who gets rewarded and why? How does it all work, and how can you work the system to your own advantage? Respecting chocolate-bearing boys notched up their hierarchy in the family ecosystem, hearing Yes, more often than No.

I respected my aunt intensely, and the raw truth is that her system of de facto governance gave her most of what she wanted in her 109 years and 11 months of life – respect, power, control, and of course, chocolate. Yet, for all of us souls who stood in watch or want of her affection or approval, the unwritten rule sets created more questions than answers. If we leaned in close, we saw the patterns of behavior and reward –affection, status, and assets. Some of us became good guessers, and so we prevailed in the family system, but did becoming a good guesser make us better people? Was it a system that served her uniquely, or a model for one of us to step into and carry forward? If someone had documented her rule set and shared it with her in kindness, would it be the guidebook she wanted memorialized for our family's future?

Motive's Role in the Reach for Rules
When families are hurting, their walls of the present are papered with relational disappointments of the past. The friction and tension of today seem unsolvable, best avoided. Fear for the future is ever present. Mom and Dad just want

what's best for the kids, the marriage, and the business. The kids long for the guidebook to achieving that elusive 'what is best' status. If only there were clear protocols to predictably earn those precious and possibly rare gold stars of approval, and to feel the relief that everything will be okay.

In a family's challenging times, governance is an unspoken tangle of assumption, misunderstanding, reaction, and new actions. The same influences – expectation and outcome – summon bad behavior in self, others, and the whole of the family system.

In good times, everyone shows up, does their part or plays their role, and enjoys the fruits of the family system, relationally and financially. Kids thrive into adulthood, go to great colleges, land great jobs, marry and stay married, and of course, give birth to the golden ticket of grandkids. Then, we wake up to the real stuff of life and find ourselves on the far more common continuum stretching from mild misalignment to outright pain.

Traditional Family Governance

At some point in the growth of a family's assets, de facto governance begins to cause more friction than freedom. With wealth as an accelerant, all the fears parents can muster amplify. Will wealth cause their family members to thrive, or take a treacherous dive into entitlement, apathy, and the complexity of bad choices? The wealth creators, having overseen their self-made enterprise for decades, sense an evolving need to establish infrastructure for the long-term growth, maintenance, and distribution of the assets.

And so, the system they seek is the one they have heard about, traditional family governance. Governing rule sets are established, usually through legal structures, with methods of administration and decision-making enforced by a family trustee, non-family trustee, and/or a group of either or both.

The family governance industry offers the tools, people, and systems to carry out a family's intentions. Yet it's the family who chooses if, when, or how to enter and leverage the system. The family also sets forth prescribed outcomes, either by default or intention.

This journey begins with a question. What are you running away from, or running towards? Are you running from the terror of potential chaos around kids with wealth? Or are you running to a system of learning, empowerment, and clear metrics for success in the family system?

Governing rule sets established with a strong wind of fear at your back propel the exact outcomes matriarchs and patriarchs fear most for their cherished relationships. They are the world's largest magnet for failure to thrive, rebellion, even trickery, and the list goes on. Fear breeds fear, getting messier by the moment.

Rule sets likewise have the power to become a multi-generational creed that empowers each individual to realize their full potential, and become a thriving contributor to the family system. They can establish clear metrics for success and clear consequences for authentic missteps.

Will family members embrace your servant leadership as an apprenticeship to their own greatness, or will they receive it as a system of dictatorship, with little chance to step out of the big dark shadow of yours? Let's look at the additional factors and actions that influence active governance work, and how increased awareness impacts the family's financial and relational outcomes.

Guard Rails' Slippery Slope

Guard rails are rules installed by one person or a group to protect another group from themselves or the outside world. The establishment of rules comes from a caring, loving place. Yet there are toxic byproducts that must be brought to the forefront of conversation. Rules are easy to place on others, yet no one wants to be ruled. A self-made matriarch or patriarch might say they have earned their stripes; it's their right to govern the assets. We simply ask, "What outcome are you governing to, and how will you feel on arrival?"

- What are you hoping to rule, or rule out?
- Are you running away from something that already happened, or could happen?
- Are you running towards something that would bring joy and impact to the family system?

Forgive my soapbox of candor for a minute. The intensity of my words are a hug of compassion driven by decades of observing the byproducts of a quintessential fork in a family's multi-generational road. When family governance work is used to create prevention guard rails, it tells your family you don't trust them to make good choices. You have begun with the end in mind, and communicated your worst fears, telling them, "There is enough of a chance that you will so royally screw up, that we had to hire people and create documents to deal with what happens when you do." Ouch. That is not what you intended to communicate, is it?

Yet now, the irony takes center stage. The psychological construct of negativity bias tells your heirs' brains to allocate more bandwidth to bad things than good things. It stacks the deck against the kid who could thrive or dive. Even worse, it converts good kids to rebels, "I'll never be good enough anyway. No matter what I do, I can never please you." If they are likely to fail in the system, why not try to outrun it, outsmart it, or at least disdain it?

Steer Clear of Arbitrary Rule Sets

As a lawyer, I'll give myself permission for generalization about my own profession. The legal system in our country often greets governance with a recycled checklist of arbitrary rule sets. When a kid turns a certain age, they get X, when they graduate, they get Y. If they marry and stay that way – or rise to a certain title in the family business – they get a great big Z on the scorecard that deposits wealth into their worlds. Matriarchs and patriarchs might ask themselves how these ages and stages predetermine an heir's readiness for the role and responsibility of wealth holder and handler. Could you create a different rule set? Could the family co-design success metrics that celebrate your family uniquely?

Governance's Digital Trend: A Slippery Slope

Organizations have begun building digital frameworks for the ongoing maintenance of governance systems. Using automated project management interfaces, there are Zoom calls, and tracking and tracing of commitments to each other, or to active projects, such as philanthropy. It's efficient for managing logistics, and for times of ease in the family system. When friction or conflict bubbles up even a little bit, remote synergy-building is unlikely to be effective.

Device screens are a callous to full participation. The safe place of hearing and vulnerability happens in a 3D environment where full humans are fully present. Countless studies about teamwork have examined interpersonal outcomes achieved digitally compared to in-person. They repeatedly point back to the size of the group and the importance of the topic. Groups and topics that matter go deeper and sustain their learning when the work is done in full company of one another. Travel is more than just inconvenient these days, it's a mess. Yet maybe, it is sometimes worth sludging through to navigate the journey to family thriving.

Begin With the End in Mind:
What Are You Bringing to the Governance Table?
On the journey to safeguard their cherished assets and relationships, matriarchs, patriarchs and other family members encounter concern or fear. The source material has one or more of the following origins:

- The memory of making a mistake and not wanting others to experience the same pain.
- Witnessing mistakes in other families alongside the terrible outcomes of their mistakes.
- A fear of unknown outcomes, and the desire to pre-empt or prevent them.

The irony continues. Much of family wealth in our country is created through entrepreneurship, a journey, which is a school of hard knocks. Find me a self-made patriarch or matriarch who hasn't failed, and I'll show you one who has yet to embrace the splendor of their mistakes. In the thousands of families we have counseled, and mine and Steve's own journeys as business owners, the worst of times often breeds the best of times. Burning the forest invites new growth. We have to let our kids – young adults or veritable adults – go out into their own big worlds and screw up sometimes. Then, we can be there to tell the stories of our failures, tools of compassion and mentorship to build strength and character in the beings that define our family's future.

We can use these experiences to invite their full bloom of potential, individually, and as contributors to the family system. We can empower them to become good decision makers and compassionate members of their own family systems, of a society that needs their thriving.

HEAR FROM JOE: AUDIO OVERVIEW #5

If a family wants their governance framework to encourage learning and empowerment – to create rule sets that educate, empower, and motivate their heirs – it is imperative to honor the pre-work.

At any given stage in the family's lifecycle, the family sits somewhere on a continuum of how things are working in the present, from ease to friction to conflict, or even toxicity. The battle scars of toxicity are at one extreme: the family holiday dinner, flooded with wine, and a rush to how-soon-can-we-leave. At other times, we may have a sense that things are a bit off. An individual, or a few members, are having a particularly hard year with each other, or several individuals are navigating a rough spot in their life journey.

Show me a mature system of relationships with some level of transparency to delicate issues, and I'll show you the tender nuance that can mobilize real change. What you bring to the governance journey directly and powerfully impacts your financial and relational outcomes of the work. Whether the friction meter is at a high or low point, the family makes a choice about whether to clear things up prior to creating their infrastructure.

Rule sets can be positive when designed from a clean heart. Humans adore clear expectations. "What do I have to do to get what I want, receive approval, or greet the next milestone?" Governance infrastructure can be a family's guidebook for individual and collective success.

The contemplative questions below offer early pre-work to test in private, on your own, or with others. Show up for the contemplation ready to hear and articulate unspoken observations in yourself and other people, and to discover dynamics you influence, yet aren't aware of.

- What blind spots could you bravely uncover to increase awareness about your current, de facto style of governance?
- What cause and effect dynamics might you become tenderly candid about?
- When you unpack the topics above, what learning will you harvest for the road ahead?

Warren and Sharon Murphy

"Our journey with Joe began with my mom's estate. She had a sizeable situation with absolutely no financial or estate planning in place. She didn't want to be involved so it came down to me to work through it all. At the time, we had great investment and insurance advisors who I had worked with on my own planning, so it made sense to reach out to them for guidance.

I explained to the advisors that if I didn't intervene, she was likely to give everything to the guide dogs for the blind. They found an attorney for us to work with who was able to put together an extensive estate plan. It was a little confusing, to say the least, but it promised to save a lot of taxes down the road.

The attorney was brilliant and certainly meant well, but he was difficult to understand. The communication was really cumbersome. After working with him for three or four years, we realized he didn't have any infrastructure in terms of a team, or even technology backups. A number of things went south, and we wound up left to our own devices trying to piece everything back together.

By this time, our original advisors had begun partnering with Joe on some of their other client families. So fortunately, this became our lifeline. And of course, my first questions were about the structure of his team, his business systems and processes, and the privacy and safety of our information. I wish I had vetted those questions more carefully before settling in with the previous attorney.

Luckily, Joe and his crew understood entirely what was going on with the existing legal work and were able to pick things up and move us forward. We quickly found that we could rely on them to get things done in a hurry and he explained everything very well. He was easy to communicate with and he was really engaged in the dialogue. We call him our big teddy bear. When my mom passed away, it was time to implement all these plans that we had worked on, and get them to work, and sure enough, Joe stepped right in there and was able to do every bit of it.

I tend to hit a stress wall even today with this kind of work and Joe is a master at getting us back to the basics of what *we are doing and why. Knowing that we have him as our sounding board alleviates so much stress. For us, being clear on the type of relationship we need is really important. It makes us more content with our results rather than feeling like we settled on a plan just to get through it and get it done.*

In prior advisory relationships, I had prioritized finding someone really smart. You also have to be able to understand what they are talking about, and more importantly, they have to take the time to understand you and your family. They have to be running a real business, not a sole practitioner type situation. There is too much at stake for it to live in one brain.

In our experience, a lot of advisors prefer an arm's-length arrangement. You're not quite sure what you can say to them because they like to keep it all business. We're the opposite. We like to have a personal relationship, where you can sit down and have a cocktail with them and think things through.

We also know that we like to see options. Sometimes you're trying to go down a path and you just need someone to slow you down for a minute and talk through your choices. And we value candor. If we had advisors who just agreed with us, we'd be in a lesser place, on the financial and legal sides, but also our ability to feel at peace about everything.

The most important thing we can say to other families is not to be content with something that you are not happy with. You have to spend some time getting to know your advisors, to learn their professional specialties but also their personal interests, and the challenges they face. We're not saying it's easy. There's a lot of learning and time that goes into finding the right fit initially. Then, you also have to continue working on the relationships with your advisors, no different than any important relationship.

*I think for families who don't feel like they have this level
of relationship or support, sometimes you don't realize the
difference that it can make. You have to have people who you
can count on. And we have that now."*

The Four Phases of Family Thriving

The nail-a-challenge gene sits proudly in the DNA of every
successful entrepreneur. This work is simply your next big
web of complexity to conquer. You may find its payoff even
more rewarding than the dopamine rush of a thriving
business.

The Four Phases of Family Thriving is our model for
helping families discover their full potential and be students
of their individual and collective thriving throughout the
seasons of life. There are plenty of models out there, some
likely better, or different than ours. Our hope is that you
seek a model on purpose, and then choose your actions
with decisive vigor. Allow the care for your family ecosystem
to mirror the soul-deep love you have for your family
members.

Some families reading this will have already begun a formal
governance journey. Others may be contemplating the
timing and trajectory of its potential. By separating the
touchstones into bite-size pieces, families can choose to
embrace one or more elements in any relevant order and
perhaps multiple phases simultaneously.

HEAR FROM JOE: AUDIO OVERVIEW #6

The Four Phases of Family Thriving

Phase One: Vet for Progress; identify where you are on the journey – from ease to friction, conflict, or toxicity – and commit to a shift.

Phase Two: Harvest Hope; existing or restored ease creates potential for expansion.

Phase Three: Choose Your Stewardship; conduct family alignment work or Family Synergy Work.

Phase Four: Govern Your Governance; continue de facto self-governing, or better yet, seek external governance advisory support, and convert your de facto rule sets to documented constructs, or partner with your governance advisors to create new rule sets.

Phase One: Vet for Progress
The family intentionally identifies its place on the continuum from toxicity to conflict, to friction to ease. Then, it makes an equally conscious choice about whether to address the status quo or let it live in the background moving into governance work.

Toxicity is an Invisible Guest who loves to muscle its way into family dynamics. Lurking in the shadows, it gobbles up the canapes and gulps down the good Scotch, wiping its mouth with a family's pain and angst. It is nefarious in its ability to normalize friction and unhealthy patterns. Toxicity has the power to taint everything that matters deeply to a loving family.

It shows up as present-day angst. Yet, its source material is historic, a complex matrix of prior misunderstanding of facts and motives. People do things on purpose or inadvertently and others react, sometimes with poor behavior. All parties carefully stockpile assumptions of the underlying influences and patterns that came before, during, or after the bad outcomes. It is easy to be an expert about someone else's drivers. Toxicity becomes a coveted rule set for how to protect, deflect, defend, or hide, in the family system.

Brené Brown has a great metaphor for the impact of toxicity on relational systems. While her focus is corporate work, the metaphor applies to any group who wants to do better together. She explains that people misperceive an ability to keep the sources of toxicity in Pandora's Box, safely latched, with the key in a forgotten hiding place. In reality, if toxicity is present, Pandora's Box has been open the whole time and the family is living in a broken system every day. It is not if you choose to deal with it, it is how, or when. Like many things in life, lack of action is still a choice.

Importantly, doing the intentional work of clearing toxicity doesn't mean you have to dance through the streets of Rome naked with your most private secrets Sharpie-ed across your forehead. It is about doing what you can at the moment, a little or a lot, celebrating the wins of progress, and noticing if, or when you are ready for more.

Phase Two: Harvest Hope
Candor in phase one pops the champagne cork of potential in phase two. Restored ease creates an environment in which everyone wants to do well together, for their own benefit, and the family system.

Importantly, when an unexpected threat hits a healthy system, the system prevails. If you are blasting down the freeway of life at 105mph, and a tire blows, you slow everything down together. Ease is your emergency kit at-the-ready, to repair and restore your journey.

Phase Three: Choose Your Stewardship
Now that you have done the good work of increasing awareness, you are ready to choose the type and depth of stewardship to bring into the family governance work.

Family alignment work is provided by many governance firms as a complement to governance's structural development. Great governance advisors have a way to peer into the souls of their client families and enhance the value of the structural system. Alignment work is effective for families who feel like they are doing just fine and believe their current ease will get them to the rule sets and structure they seek. It is also a solution for families who know they suffer from toxicity yet prefer to not address it prior to seeking governance support, or for whom traditional therapy and governance are pursued in tandem. Let's revisit together our nomenclature for the use of data in solving problems.

No Data: the family and the governance advisors step straight into infrastructure development without exploring the qualitative state of the family system.

Stated Data: the governance advisors do the good work of curiosity, learning what makes a family joyful, and where their weak spots and pain points slow things down.

Verified Data: the family is so juiced up by their restored ease, they are inclined to further explore nuanced relational dynamics, cementing their traditional governance foundation.

Verified Data uses awareness as fuel for the betterment of the family ecosystem. Consider all those times in business when you are faced with a strategic decision. If you are balled up in angst and emotion, it puts a dark haze over your instincts. Yet, facing that same decision from a clear, quiet place of your best self, the people and economics prevail.

- You see all the factors, upsides and downsides, and future impact of each.
- You are more willing and likely to see and consider new data points.
- You find yourself inviting other people's perceptions and opinions to the table with authenticity over obligation.
- You make elegant, balanced choices.

Family synergy work is outcome-driven both economically and interpersonally. Healthy family systems steeped in self- and other-awareness achieve more effective and lasting financial and relational governance results. Synergy offers the gift of nuance, those tiny pearls of wisdom or insight that catalyze huge shifts. For every big family decision there are dozens if not hundreds of them. It turns out nuance has greater impact on outcomes than the big obvious stuff sitting under a strobe light marked, 'Deal with this.'

Synergistic families create learning agility together. They know when to pause and breathe deeply, and how to ask great questions of each other. They practice curiosity as a discipline not an obligation.

Bear with me for a little sentimentality here. Create a mental picture of your grandkids or great grandkids growing up in a family environment where these tools are the norm. Imagine if these behaviors were modeled and mentored from their first observational memories, into their early words and choices. We suggest that it might impact how they begin to show up in their own little lives, and as time goes on, who they invite into the family system through friendship and marriage.

Phase Four: Govern Your Governance
This work is far from a check-the-box project. At times, families will find a slow creep of friction muscling its way back into relationships. It is often most noticeable seen through someone else's reaction or a young person's old-soul awareness.

Throughout your journey to thriving, rely on the four-phase system for intentional course corrections. If an outcome presents itself that is less than desirable, lean into curiosity. Was it a system failure, an agreement failure or both? Or perhaps it is just the stuff of life – a rogue wave of external influence that soaks you from behind. If it doesn't feel good, or it's taking an outsized amount of effort, and it happens more than once, notice where you are in the four phases. Revisit the concepts of friction, or even possible toxicity, and consider a possible tune up. Gut-check your current ability to harvest hope, and how it can influence modifications in your governance infrastructure.

Course corrections make everything easier, from planning a family vacation, to the big stuff of wealth's future footprint. They become easier over time, and often families can do their own tune ups.

Ask the following questions, or your own, with family members:

- Who or what hurts?
- How much, how often, and how deeply does it hurt?
- What are you certain can't or won't change?
- If it could change, how would it impact your family ecosystem?
- If a particular family member is hurting, what would you like them to know with unstoppable clarity, regarding your love and respect for them?

When things are going well, flip the questions and use the same litmus test.

- Who is thriving?
- How is it impacting the individual, and the family ecosystem?
- What kind of support framework can you create together to proactively sustain the thriving?
- What milestones can you celebrate?
- What emotions are you experiencing that might be difficult to articulate, yet would help sustain another's thriving: pride, gratitude, joy, respect, or admiration?

Often the deepest progress is made when family synergy is high. Motives and misunderstandings are the loose gravel of life. Collect these nuances and let them be the bricks and mortar of deeper synergy and stronger foundations.
In the end, each family makes their own choice, and that choice has the potential to be a list of your 'coulds', not your 'shoulds'. Awareness of your choices increases your discernment. All that we aspire for on your behalf is that hope is the great conversation that guides an intentional journey.

Chapter 5

Othership

Your eyes flutter open to a new day, still in that dreamy in-between state, and your intellect does its morning thing. You review the day's priorities, the relationships that need tending to and strategic initiatives that will sputter and stall without your innate wisdom. The totality would drive mere mortals back into the safe hibernation of sleep. For you, other people's problems are your morning protein shake. The most improbable strategic messes are a feast for your mental acuity, knowing you matter to things that matter most. As the financial leader in your family system, the world assigns motive to your servant's heart, calling it control or ego. Your selfless spirit couldn't be more opposite.

Welcome home. You are part of a tribe called Othership.

Othership is our way of describing and honoring the misunderstood servant leaders of the world. They are matriarchs and patriarchs, second generation wealth stewards and third generation trailblazers, single moms and philanthropists. It is people like my Zia Sarafina.

Definition of Othership
The instinct and drive to anticipate other's needs, innovating to serve and solve, often putting yourself second.

Some of you reading this will blame Othership for your own suffering. Many will dismiss the concept as an attempt to give Dad a hall pass, to justify decades of driving the business first, perhaps at the sake of his family's non-financial needs. The pre-dawn 'phone calls during family vacations, the missed Little League games and Girl Scout initiations. In this other-first dance, who defines other? It is disorienting at best and sometimes devastating. I get it. I am part of that tribe, alongside so many families we serve.

Now that candor is on the table, we tenderly offer an alternative perspective. Othership is the desire to be your best self in the relationships you cherish and the vast expanse of scenarios to which you are accountable every day. It offers a framework for understanding the roles we play in our relational ecosystems: family, business, faith, or friendships. It is a methodology to unpack the misunderstandings embedded in these roles and decipher the mixed messages we create and become a party to.

Othership offers a shift in focus – to step aside from your daily lens of what is true – and learn another's truth – how they see themselves and how they see you. It is a mirror for authenticity in your hope for a better way. How real is your longing? How sincere and deep is your want to know others differently, or more fully?

As you test this journey, curiosity is once again your trusted elixir, a tool for learning the facts and fact patterns hidden in your blind spots. It makes space for compassion and vulnerability, and – if used sincerely and not as a weapon – it is innately safe. It is the gentle inquiry, quiet question, or meaningful pause, when so often we put a cuff around the time we allow for an experience to unfold.

There are three leading roles in the family system: financial leader, family leader, and future family leaders.

The Financial Leader

In our work with successful families and business owners, we see a variety of financial leadership roles. Whether it is a self-made patriarch or matriarch, or a second-generation family member who is stewarding the growth of the wealth created in a previous generation, the leader's pressure is immense.

The financial leader is deeply accountable to keeping everyone in their orbit safe. There is no conscious decision if, when, or who. It is as ingrained in their modus operandi as breathing is to the autonomic nervous system. Even when the business or body of wealth has created more than enough, early day struggles are embedded in their muscle memory. Their habits were developed and rewarded during the worst of times. Every man or women in this role knows the middle-of-the-night terror, if three bad things happen, we are screwed. The constant attention to downside protection is a care-giving behavior, hyper vigilance is Othership in motion.

The financial leader must constantly pre-see ripple effects on vast constituent sets. Every action or decision impacts someone or something right in front of them and dozens of others standing on the field of play or sitting in the bleachers. The leader is constantly prioritizing the good of the whole based on who or what needs help.

Meanwhile, knowing the playbook outside of the business (and inside the family system) is an altogether different reality. Are the skills transferable? If not, how does the financial leader quarterback the win for a sport they haven't yet mastered?

Now, let's examine the external perspectives regarding the motives and choices of the financial leader. A reader warning, these are painful truths.

> *"Dad's business is his first-born child. He has always cared more about it than us. There is no way his drive is selfless. He loves writing the playbook and controlling what happens on the field. All he does is work. Sometimes his words and actions don't line up with what I see happening. We do not need any more money, we just want more time with him. What am I missing?"*

The Family Leader

This role is often played by the matriarch, yet it may also be the patriarch, or a second-generation sibling who stewards family harmony.

The family leader is part mediator, part apologist. She is an elder stateswoman who does not seek the limelight and never asks for credit. Let's be clear, she loves this role. Her definition of a win is helping a family member see another person or situation differently. She works behind the scenes coaching people to pick their battles and curate their timing. She does not take sides because she does not know how. Doing so would violate every rule in her other-first playbook.

Now, let's examine the external perspectives regarding the motives and choices of the family leader.

> *"Dad is eternally grateful to Mom, yet he never says it, at least not in front of us. It hurts our hearts to see Mom as powerless,*

stuck in a role she did not ask for. She is always taking someone's side and it's never mine. She puts herself second and it is painful to watch. Maybe she should put herself first more often. If there is an underlying intention or logic to it, I am not seeing it."

Future Family Leaders

Future family leaders are the adult children and succeeding generations.

Future family leaders may feel trapped in a role they didn't ask for and do not totally understand. Nobody gave them the playbook for how to be on this team. They live in the constant shadow of the financial leader's unmatchable greatness. Sometimes, all they want is to create their own rule set for freedom and success. Other times, it is easier to stay on the sidelines, conquering what is expected while nursing their injuries, hoping nobody asks too many questions regarding the source of their pain.

Now, let's examine the external perspectives regarding the motives and choices of the future family leaders.

"Mom and Dad just want you to find your own thriving. They need you to step up to the plate. We are all adults now, creating and contributing to the whole of the family. If you want to be treated differently, then join us in the game of risk and reward, relationally and financially."

Dan and Carin Baker
"When we first sought out Joe's help with estate planning and distribution, and creating a plan for the family business going forward, we knew we needed advice on the business and financial side, but I don't think we realized how much relational complexity was wrapped up in all of that.

Three of our four children were either in the business at that time or had been at one time. There were all those underlying questions, each of them wondering who's going to get what and when. Who's going to get to take over the company? Who's going to get to be the new boss?

We knew we didn't want any surprises after we were gone. We wanted them to know exactly what our plans were while we were still around to answer their questions. We didn't want them to find out what the plan was from some attorney sitting in an office when we passed.

When we began the work with Joe, two of our kids were actively working in the business. And it turns out, the way I intuitively managed that journey created the opposite of what I intended. I wanted everything to be super fair and I didn't want our kids to be competing with each other. I thought my approach would help us avoid friction and in the end the kids started to harbor resentment and even some entitlement. There were expectations that were unspoken and, in some cases, unrealistic.

The kids weren't comfortable coming to me and confronting me. So, they would go to Carin. Mom was a safer bet. Carin has been the traditional matriarch, and I've been the one running the business. She has always been so supportive of me and the work it takes to run and grow a company. She has always been the relational rock in the family. The kids would have a feeling about something happening in the business and they would go to her to talk it through.

She would try to help them see all the different sides to the situation. Even though she wasn't actively working in the business, she was their chosen sounding board. She didn't want their feelings to be hurt or for them to feel frustrated, so she would say, 'Let me talk to Dad.'

When we first started working with Joe and his teams, he suggested we all go offsite together and rent a house for a family retreat. There was a lot that needed to be said, yet I think we were all nervous about going there. We knew we had to be honest and share our feelings.

Before the retreat, Joe really emphasized the pre-work Carin and I needed to do with him. He sat with us and learned about each of our kids and the dynamics from our perspective.

When we got to the retreat, everyone was a little nervous. The kids thought we were going to sit around and look at spreadsheets the whole time. Instead, Joe was a magician in getting each one of us to share our true feelings about not just our business, but about things that were going on in our lives that were stressful and unspoken. He was so present in our conversations. We hadn't experienced that before from advisory professionals.

The weekend helped the kids understand that as parents, we had made mistakes and we would keep making them, but we were truly doing all of this for them. That even as their boss, I am their dad first. That I'm not against them, I am rooting for them. I didn't realize how afraid they were to talk to me. They thought I was too set in my ways to have the conversations.

By having those counseling experiences, it opened new doors of communication that we probably didn't think were possible, or maybe we didn't notice the doors had shut over time. Each of us got to share how we truly felt in a safe environment. That environment definitely helped us go deeper – individually and together as a family.

Joe was instrumental at guiding the conversations and giving us suggestions along the way. He took us down a road, and *paved the way, making everybody feel heard and understood. And we cried and we laughed. The experience really brought our family together.*

In retrospect, when we started the process, we didn't know what we didn't know. We never thought about something that would put the business and the long-term transition plan together with the counseling and also education.

At the end of that first retreat, Joe was very articulate that it didn't end here. If Carin and I had questions, or if the kids wanted to call him directly, he welcomed it. That gave all of us the confidence that this was the beginning of lasting change, not a one-off that would fade over time.

As a result of the journey, the kids understood both Carin and me better. I think they finally saw her heavy lift over the years, always having my back, reinforcing my confidence and supporting me. They understand how much she has trusted me through all the highs and lows. They hadn't really seen that part of our partnership before and I think it gave them a new level of respect for her role – beyond being a great mother and wife.

For other families in our shoes, we feel the most important thing is to go in with an open mind and a ton of hope. If you find the right counseling fit, you can relax and let the professional lead because they know where they are taking you even if you can't see it for yourselves. Feeling safe being guided, like someone has your back, is a very powerful experience."

The Journey to Fix the Scripts: Dialogue Cures All
Changes in communication precede changes in behavior. For the family member who is desperate to be seen differently in the family system, the journey begins in an unexpected place, Othership. It turns out that if you first seek to learn what is happening for someone else, the shifts begins almost effortlessly. Curiosity makes it safe for others to be vulnerable. If you lace up and lead with curiosity about your fellow family member's injuries, it will launch their authentic interest in yours. However, by definition, Othership teaches us that we have to want to know. False outreach, baits, switches, and hidden motives will exacerbate everyone's pain.

In an adult family system, every member must be willing to respect previous hierarchies yet no longer use them as the forever reality or an excuse for where things stand. Othership is ageless, lacking an organization chart of who is allowed to ask the questions, or be the change agent. Anyone in the system may play an active role in the desired outcomes.

Othership helps a family navigate how to be with wealth not what to do with it. When someone feels unseen or misunderstood, do they push away from relational intimacy, or feel invited to step in a little closer? Doesn't the most powerful person in the room deserve to be seen differently? Doesn't the quietest member of the family deserve to be honored and validated? Isn't each of you misunderstood and unseen in some way? Compassion is a magnet for progress where change can seem implausible.

Some people say you can't care for others until you care for yourself. Othership believes that serving selflessly is mere oxygen. Imagine how powerful a family can be when each member navigates life and roles through this filter?

Together, you become unstoppable in what you can achieve for yourself, your family, and the world at your doorstep.

Please note that we do not believe other-first and self-care are mutually exclusive. If anything, self-care can be an other-first behavior. How you eat, sleep, exercise, and repair your psyche has a decisive impact on your ability to be your best self for others. And often, you still prioritize others first in these moments.

OTHERSHIP EXERCISE

Use this exercise to think about one of your cherished relational ecosystems, whether family, business, faith, or friendships. Think of a time when you felt either, 1. Extreme joy, or 2. Extreme sorrow, pain or remorse. Grab your notebook and take some quiet time to answer these questions.

- What happened?
- What instincts were in motion?
- What did you successfully anticipate?
- What surprised or blindsided you?
- Which dominoes fell first?
- What were your needs in this situation?
- What were the other participants' needs?
- What did you see or solve?
- What do you wish you could have seen more clearly or solved differently?
- Did you put yourself first or others first?
- How did it feel?

NEXT GENERATION OTHERSHIP
EXERCISE

In the inter-generational shadow of misunderstanding, this exercise is an olive branch to mutual curiosity and compassionate dialogue. It is designed for adult children in a family system.

Complete this exercise in two phases. First, pose the question in private, imagining the dialogue in your mind's eye. Second, invite a live conversation with the same person. Choose a mutually safe environment for each phase.

Questions for the financial leader
- How did you first know you were meant to lead and grow the business and/or body of wealth?
- What was the most painful mistake you made early on? What did you learn from it?
- Why did you prevail when others on similar quests did not?
- What was the hardest thing you ever did, or the toughest decision you ever made?
- Why do you keep driving so hard when we seem to have more than we need?
- How can I be more supportive of you and our family ecosystem?
- Finish by sharing what you respect most about the financial leader. Ask them to share what they respect most about you.

Questions for the family leader
- What is your favorite aspect of your role in our family?
- In what areas do you feel misunderstood?
- If you could make one wish for each of us adult kids,

what would they be?
- Why do you put up with so much pain and pressure in our family?
- What do you regret?
- What do you still hope for everyday?
- Finish by sharing what you respect most about the family leader. Ask them to share what they respect most about you.

HEAR FROM JOE: AUDIO OVERVIEW #7

Level V Curiosity

Level V curiosity is part concept, part training regime for new relational muscle memory. Just as humans' greatest threat is the fear of loss of connection, curiosity offers equilibrium. It seeks harmony and common ground, the real kind, not the Band-Aid of, "Let's just get through this." You discover compassion for others who are experiencing something you have never had to deal with. You realize that, perhaps, you have been in the shoes of the person you are most inclined to judge, absent awareness of your solidarity.

The Power of Level V Curiosity

- It prioritizes learning something new over being right about what you already know.
- When you listen for what you don't know, your hearing improves.
- Deep curiosity is most challenging when you are under immense pressure.
- Relational and financial ecosystems thrive as open systems, inviting more data and unexplored possibilities.

- New information can powerfully dismantle prior misunderstandings, increasing awareness of underlying motive.

Level V curiosity slows things down and reveals disparate perspectives. The logic of the situation grounds us back to what is possible. When we are certain we are right, it sucks the oxygen out of a conversation that hasn't yet started. We must give up the staunch search for proof and become interested in our blind spots. Angst and pressure dissolve, revealing a room lined with open doors, each offering the hope of previously unseen possibilities.

Curiosity is an authentic emotion. It knows whether you are being truthful to yourself and others. It knows if and how much you seek to understand a perspective that is so far outside of your own assumption, even your own wheelhouse.

The Top Five Scenarios That Block Level V Curiosity
- In a hurry
- Exhausted
- Too much to lose
- Position or reputation to protect
- Too close to it

Just when you are certain that you are already more curious than most – that all of this is other people's plight – know this: the smarter, faster thinker suffers more. Yep. The most intelligent, street-smart, educated, and technically-trained person in the room is most likely to bypass the questions. Curiosity becomes compartmentalized, something you already did in areas you already excel. The more intuitive souls find it easier to reach Level V.

LEVEL V CURIOSITY EXERCISE

Here is a universal truth. We are all wrong at least once in our cherished relationships. When you own the possibility of being mistaken, it disarms the situation and all the parties to the outcome.

This exercise has three motives: own your perspective, ask for help, and hear past what you already know.
Select a situation or relationship in which you feel soul-deep certainty – that your take on things is accurate – and that your perspective is likely wiser and more evolved than other parties to the situation.

- What do I absolutely know to be true?
- What would others in the inner circle say that is fundamentally inaccurate?
- How is perspective or lack of alignment affecting the situation?
- Why do they think or feel that way?
- What am I missing?
- Who should I talk to first?

Care to Know™

In our counseling and our teaching, Care to Know™ is our lifeblood for seeing to the left and right of the thing in front of us. It reminds us that the real problem is likely hovering at 10,000 feet above, or buried deep in minutia of financial, legal, tax, and relational cobwebs.

The world comes at you faster than ever in the history of our humanity. There is literally not enough physical time or intellectual bandwidth to tend to everyone and everything that deserves your focus. We pose a tender question. What do you have to give up to get what you want?

Care to Know™ is about financial leaders, family leaders, and future family leaders choosing to create more space for dialogue with their families and advisors. It is encouraging each other to step outside the comfort zone of your innate wisdom to seek what you don't already know or haven't yet learned.

Care to Know™ is a shift from, I Know, to I Think. The search for efficiency is a Petri dish for misunderstanding. Pre-conversation certainty will get it done quickly, whatever the 'it' of that day is. However, it will not fully invite or solve the problem. It is akin to using a zoom lens yet leaving the lens cap firmly in place. What are you missing? I Think is the shift from organizing the I Know data you already have, to inviting the data points you do not even know exist. To savoring the options, inviting push back and offering it to others, knowing that together you can prevail.

CARE TO KNOW™ EXERCISE

Think of a person or scenario that matters deeply. Jot down ten things you know to be true about them or it. Next, flip each of your knowings to questions on the journey to I Think. See the examples below.

I Know	I Think
Johnny will never work hard enough, at least not as hard as I do.	He hasn't found his passion. How could I help him explore possibilities without feeling shadowed or judged?
I don't need to question my trusted advisors. That's why I trust them.	What deeper solutions might surface if I invited everyone to play in the sandbox, showing up this way myself, and asking and inviting others to do the same?
I don't have bandwidth to stop and contemplate the obvious. I need to move on so I can put out the next fire.	Getting to the root of a problem is my superpower. Where have I yet to offer it?
They will never understand that I am doing it all for them.	How can I possibly explain how hard it is to slow down? How can I ask for the grace to learn how?
My spouse is my rock. They know this. It is obvious.	Have I said it out loud lately to my spouse? Have I ever said it in front of the kids?

At the end of the day, remember that you already have the skills to broaden your perspective and invite others to join you. In fact, these skills are the quintessential part of your best decisions, and your proudest moments of mentorship. They are the quiet pride of an other-first world.

"There's no limit to what can be accomplished when it doesn't matter who gets the credit."

Ralph Waldo Emerson

Epilogue

Some folks are okay with the status quo. If an important professional or personal relationship isn't working, it's simply the stuff of life. Relational change is difficult, especially when there is no framework to transform the current malaise.

Pause for a moment and conduct an intellectual inventory of your professional advisory team. How did each of them wind up at your table? Why do they stay? Is it synergy, joy, power, ego, complacency, or financial gain? Are the drivers yours, theirs, or a little of each?

Conduct the same inventory of your family or personal relationships. Are you tolerating, or celebrating the people who matter most?

In both camps, how are you showing up? Own curiosity as your first reaction. Your material assets and cherished relationships have vast potential. How are you tapping it? In what ways are you empowering or limiting the outcomes you seek? If a more satisfying dynamic is closer than you think, will you make the journey? Will you muster your innate grit to nurture, celebrate, and build a thriving tribe?

Imagine that next time you wake up with an idea that is percolating at Mach speed, on the verge of something big, you call one of your trusted advisors. They respond unexpectedly, with questions absent of judgment or advice, tossing contemplation into your intellectual sandpit. Your unpolished thinking expands without limits, shifting and forming the best version of your big idea.

How did your behavior invite their deeper thinking to the conversation?

Results matter. Yet, when you show up fully with, and for, the people who create them, outcomes exceed prior possibility. Everyone feels heard, honored, and challenged.

Care to Know™ is part methodology, part call to action. We are imperfect beings living in a fractured system of life with wealth. We can eliminate angst and pain, and mitigate its recurrence, yet doing so is a team sport. Each player is essential and no single team member can win on their own.

We must no longer lean on sheer will to push and prevail through middle grounds and status quos. Instead, we can cherish our blind spots and learn our motives. When we Care to Know™ others' motives, not simply as raw material for negotiating outcomes, we become curious for the good of each stakeholder and the health of the tribe.

Next time you find yourself blocking and tackling through life with wealth, make space for pause. What are you blocking? Is your tackling causing others to tuck away their pain or wisdom? What if, instead, you walk into these rooms with affection for better alternatives?

You know how to mentor others to be their best selves. You do this work of servant leadership every day. Make a list of the important relationships whose thriving matters. Give your list a name. Care to Know™. Make it a promise.

- I will ask.
- I will hear.
- I will hold hope for change and expansion.

This work is not only about fixing doom and gloom. When we tolerate neutral relationships, we relinquish potential. Instead, you can rally your innate courage to vet, steward, encourage, and discern; to surround yourself with mutual thriving.

And so, we invite you to join us on a mutual journey. As we noted at the beginning, this book is dedicated to Othership. Othership is the instinct and drive to anticipate other's needs, innovating to serve and solve, often putting yourself second.

If our thinking and exercises resonate, you are part of this servant leader tribe. Let's walk forward together ...

The Othership Institute
Creating a place to think for successful families and business owners.
• Facilitated forums.
• Private retreats.
• A safe place for candor and curiosity.
• A methodology to maximize your tribe's potential.

via The Othership Community
at www.strazzerizimancini.com/othership

"*Never confuse movement with action.*"
Ralph Waldo Emerson

Motive's Creed

- Pose deep and difficult questions to yourself and others prior to choosing or being chosen.

- Vet relational potential with commensurate vigor for what's at stake in the relationship.

- Use quantifiable metrics to evaluate alignment.

- Bring a willingness to show up differently, revealing more, or releasing attachment to personal gain.

- Replace complacency with stewardship, annually and into the twilight of your relationships.

- Invite curiosity and vulnerability to be your partners in discovering the brilliance of unexpected outcomes.

- Peer inside for self-learning: what are you willing to give up to get what you want?

Contact The Author

If this book has helped you and you want to contact the author, please go to any of the following platforms.

Learn More QR Code:

Othership Institute website:
www.strazzerimancini.com/othership

Facebook online community:
www.facebook.com/StrazzeriMancini/

YouTube Channel:
www.youtube.com/@strazzerimancini

LinkedIn:
www.linkedin.com/in/joestrazzeri/

Instagram:
www.instagram.com/joe.strazzeri.77/

Links to these resources can also be found on the author's website: www.caretoknow.info

Quotation References

Chapter 1
- Steve Jobs: 1955 – 2011: American businessman, inventor and investor best known for co-founding the technology company Apple Inc.

Chapter 2
- *The Molecule of More*, Dr Daniel Z Lieberman and Micheal E Long, BenBella Books, 2018
- Nancy Sinatra: American actress, singer, film producer and author, eldest daughter of Frank and Nancy Sinatra, best known for her 1965 signature hit song, *These Boots Are Made for Walkin'*
- Eric Clapton: English guitarist, and singer-songwriter, *Before You Accuse Me*, 1989
- *Good to Great*, Jim Collins, HarperCollins, 2001

Chapter 3
- Lord Acton: 19th century British historian and writer
- Ronald Reagan: American politician and actor, 40th president of the United States from 1981 to 1989
- Frank Braglin: American business mentor

Chapter 4
- Brené Brown: American academic, podcaster and author of six number-one New York Times bestselling books

Chapter 5
- Ralph Waldo Emerson: American essayist, lecturer, philosopher, minister, abolitionist and poet, who led the Transcendentalist movement of the mid-19th century

Notes

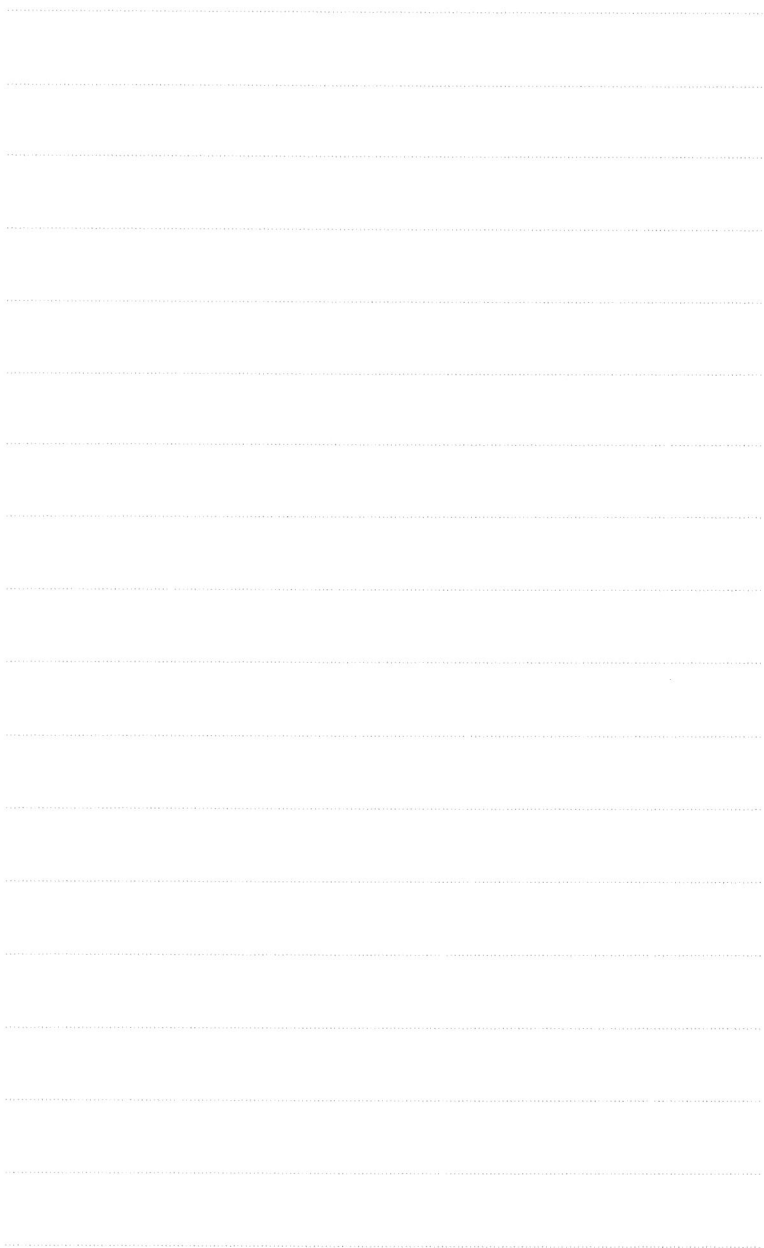